'ITCHING AFTER RHYME'

'ITCHING AFTER RHYME'
A Life of John Clare

ARNOLD CLAY

PARAPRESS LTD
TUNBRIDGE WELLS

ISBN: 1-898594-68-6

First published in the UK by
PARAPRESS LTD
5 Bentham Hill House
Stockland Green Road
Tunbridge Wells
Kent
TN3 0TJ

A catalogue record for this book is available
from the British Library

Printed in Great Britain by
Biddles Ltd, Guildford and King's Lynn

Typeset in Aldus by Vitaset, Paddock Wood

Contents

Illustrations

Colour plates between pages 50 and 51

Plates between pages 82 and 83

Plate no. 3, photogravure plates 13-16 and the landscapes on the cover are by Peter Moyse. Other photographs are by the author.

Textual Note

The texts of Clare's writings have always presented a problem. He never mastered orthodox spelling and punctuation. In the passages quoted in this book, a space is left where there should have been a full stop, and Clare's original spelling and punctuation (or lack of it) has been retained.

Acknowledgements

Quotations from the poetry and prose of John Clare are reproduced with permission of Curtis Brown Ltd., London, on behalf of Eric Robinson. Copyright Eric Robinson 1985, 1988, 1996.

The portrait of John Clare by William Hilton (detail) used on the cover is by courtesy of the National Portrait Gallery, London.

The bust by Henry Behnes, the painting of 1844 by Thomas Grimshaw, and the drawing by George Maine of 1848 are reproduced by kind permission of Northamptonshire Libraries and Information Service.

Grateful thanks to Peter Moyse of the John Clare Society for the free use of his photographs, on the cover and in the plates.

… I used to rove
Thro burghley park that darksome grove
Of limes where twilight lingered grey
Like evening in the midst of day
And felt without a single skill
That instinct that would not be still
To think of song sublime beneath
That heaved my bosom like my breath
That burned and chilled and went and came
Without or uttering or a name
Until the vision waked with time
And left me itching after rhyme

from 'The Progress of Rhyme'

Introduction

John Clare is one of the greatest poets of English rural life. The son of a farm-labourer, he worked as a thresher, labourer and gardener. His formal education, such as it was, ended at the age of eleven, but he had a thirst for knowledge and became a model example of the self-taught man. In 1820 he rose to fame as the Northamptonshire Peasant Poet with the publication of his *Poems Descriptive of Rural Life and Scenery*. From that time it was clear that England had a new and very original poet, but the public's enthusiasm was short-lived, and each new volume – *The Village Minstrel* (1821), *The Shepherd's Calendar* (1827) and *The Rural Muse* (1835) – met with diminishing applause. His work was soon forgotten by all but a few admirers. Feelings of inferiority and insecurity, and the constant struggle against poverty, contributed to his mental breakdown. He was admitted to an asylum at High Beach, Epping Forest, in 1837, where he was a voluntary patient. He 'escaped' in 1841 and, after a few months at home, he was taken to the Northamptonshire General Lunatic Asylum where he spent the last twenty-three years of his life, still writing prolifically and drawing inspiration from nature.

Clare's life spanned one of the great ages of English poetry – the Romantic age of Blake, Wordsworth, Byron, Shelley and

Keats, whose writing began to flourish as political and social revolutions were sweeping through Europe. Clare's true class identity has been widely debated, with some critics maintaining that it is patronising to view him as a mere 'peasant' poet, while others have regarded his social status as intrinsic to the kind of verse he wrote. Similarly, there have been concerted efforts to place him within the tradition of the Romantic movement.

This movement represented a violent reaction to the political, social and intellectual climate of the eighteenth century. It seemed to signal the victory of liberty over tyranny in a time of change, when accepted norms were being questioned and tested; contrarily it was an age in which privilege and oppression had been reasserted in England by a series of Tory governments. Clare's life reflected both the opportunities and the frustrations which faced a man of his class and generation.

Human beings of all classes were seen by the Romantics as individuals rather than simply members of society – individuals whose emotional responses were more important than their intellectual arguments. They gave voice to sentiments, desires and unconscious feelings in a way that reverberates in the modern mind. 'All good poetry', wrote Wordsworth, 'is the spontaneous overflow of powerful feelings.' The English romantic poets, especially Wordsworth, Keats and Shelley, expressed a profound response to the natural world, under threat by mass industrialisation (which included the industrialisation of agriculture), and this informed much of their finest work. This threat has not gone away; rather its scale has become more ominous, and its scope has widened to embrace the whole globe.

Although it is only just to Clare to place him in the Romantic framework, we should perhaps argue that his poetry can be valued in its own right, and outside of his own time. Of all the great poets of his age, Clare lived closest to nature, and most closely felt the effects of social change. He observed at first hand, and felt at first hand too, both the destruction of the natural scene, and of the class which lived with it and from it. This is one reason why his individual voice should be especially valued, but there are further reasons.

His poetic responses were different from the other Romantic poets. A great deal of his poetry is descriptive, and though no description can ever be neutral, there is often a marked attempt to describe things for their own sake:

> I love the fitfull gusts that shakes
>   The casement all the day
> And from the mossy elm tree takes
>   The faded leaf away
> Twirling it by the window pane
> With thousand others down the lane
>
> I love to see the shaking twig
>   Dance til the shut of eve
> The sparrow on the cottage rig
>   Whose chirp would make believe
> That spring was just now flirting by
> In summers lap with flowers to lie[1]

He has the eye of a nineteenth-century naturalist, almost of a scientist:

> Insects of misterious birth
>   Sudden struck my wondering sight
> Doubtless brought by moister forth
>   Hid in notts of spittle white

Backs of leaves the burthen bears
  Where the sunbeams cannot stray
Wood sears called that wet declares
  So the knowing shepherds say[2]

Contemporary critics sometimes begged Clare to put in more 'philosophy' and complained that his poems were too unremittingly 'descriptive'. Even though dismayed by suffering in later life, Clare simply made a straightforward, first-hand analysis of the social and moral issues around him. When he was shut out by destiny and the hand of man from his own physical worlds, he lived within the memory of them, and found consolation in his own form of Christianity.

Clare's lack of 'philosophical' perspective sprang from the choices he made during his self-education. He is largely uncluttered with metaphysical baggage. He wrote of what he saw, not what he thought he ought to see. Although he achieved little recognition in his lifetime, subsequent generations have discovered with pleasure the robustness and sensitivity of his writing. Today his poetry is being read for its freshness of tone and its pleasant rural detail. He knew every inch of his native landscape and wrote of it passionately, as in 'Emmonsales Heath'

O who can pass such lovely spots
Without a wish to stray
And leave life's cares a while forgot
To muse an hour away

Ive often met with places rude
Nor failed their sweet to share
But passed an hour with solitude
And left my blessing there[3]

His description of 'The Setting Sun' shows how simply and easily he associated the natural with the spiritual:

> This scene how beauteous to the musing mind
> That now swift slides from my enchanting view
> The Sun sweet setting yon far hills behind
> In other worlds his Visits to renew
> What spangling glories all around him shine
> What nameless colours cloudless and serene
> (A heavenly prospect brightest in decline)
> Attend his exit from this lovly scene –
> – So sets the christians sun in glories clear
> So shines his soul at his departure here
> No clouding doubts nor misty fears arise
> To dim hopes golden rays of being forgiven
> His sun sweet setting in the clearest skyes
> In safe assurance wings the soul to heaven –

Clare's descriptions of the landscape, of birds and animals, the seasons and the daily life of a Northamptonshire village just before the Industrial Revolution, are among the finest of such accounts in English literature. From its ecology to its working practices, he gives us an authentic view of rural England at the start of its gradual disappearance in the face of urban development and agricultural revolutions both old and new. His poems are full of insights which challenge us to protect and conserve for future generations, so that he should be regarded as one of the enduring and true Romantics, who speaks as much for the twenty-first century as he did for his own.

In addition to his own autobiographical writings – his *Sketches in the Life of John Clare by Himself*, 'Autobiographical

Fragments', his 'Journal', and his famous 'Journey out of Essex' – there have been a number of lives of John Clare. The first was Frederick Martin's, first published in 1865, the year after Clare's death. This was followed in 1873 by J.L. Cherry's *Life and Remains of John Clare*. The next life, published in 1932 (revised in 1972) was the work of two champions of Clare's poetry: J.W. and Anne Tibble, *John Clare: A Life*, followed in 1951 by June Wilson's *Green Shadows*. Another biography, by Edward Storey, *A Right to Song: The Life of John Clare*, was published in 1982.

Sadly, these lives are now out of print – therefore no full-scale biography of Clare is currently available. This short contribution is a modest attempt to 'fill the gap'. The life of John Clare was an extraordinary one; indeed, so extraordinary was it that its story sometimes seems to have eclipsed the interest in his poetry. However, there are good reasons for maintaining an interest in Clare's life in tandem with an interest in his work – and that is my reason for writing this book. It is not a work of literary criticism, but a 'popular' biography. Using as principal sources Clare's own autobiographical writings, I have told his story for those who have only heard of him and want to know more, in the hope that it will lead to a wider and deeper knowledge of this remarkable poet.

ARNOLD CLAY
January 2000

NOTES

1. Oxford Authors: *John Clare* (ed. by Eric Robinson and David Powell), page 382
2. *Ibid.* page 57
3. *Ibid.* page 182
4. *Ibid.* page 6

CHAPTER 1

A Country Childhood

Half way between Peterborough and Stamford, on the edge of the Cambridgeshire fens, lies the village of Helpston. It is a long, spacious village, its centre being at the crossing of two roads, with houses straggling in all directions into the wide, flat countryside. At the end of the eighteenth century Helpston's population of 270 consisted of families, mostly poor and uneducated people, who worked on the land. The village had its own complement of tradesmen: butcher, shoemaker, stone-mason, blacksmith, wheelwright and publican. Tradesmen in neighbouring villages were busily engaged in their own industries. People came from other parishes to share in Helpston's feasts and fairs: a few gypsies were tolerated on their traditional camping sites; otherwise it was not a place to attract many visitors.

Into this village, somewhere between 1761 and 1764, there came a young man, reputed to be a Scotsman by birth and a good fiddle-player by way of an entertainer, who went under the name of John Donald Parker. He was an itinerant schoolmaster, and stayed in Helpston long enough to run a school in the church vestry. During his leisure hours he courted Alice Clare, the parish clerk's daughter; but when she gave him the news that she was bearing his child, he disappeared from the village and was never heard of again. She does not seem to have felt any bitterness against the man who deserted her, because she gave their son his surname, Parker, as his first name.

Such was Parker Clare's entry into the world on 14th January 1765. He became a casual farm worker, and at the age of twenty-six started courting Ann Stimson, whose father was a shepherd in the nearby village of Castor. They married in December 1792, and Parker Clare took his young bride home to Helpston, where they lived in a thatched cottage in the village street which runs south from the crossroads.

By now Ann was two months pregnant, and on 13th July 1793 she gave birth to twins – a boy and a girl. The girl (Bessy), although a much stronger baby than her brother, died soon after her birth, but John – a pint-sized creature 'of a waukly constitution'[1] – survived. Ann Clare had two more children: Elizabeth, who was born in July 1796, and Sophy in April 1798. Elizabeth died in childhood, leaving John with his youngest sister for company.

John was never a strong child, and he needed all the care that his parents were able to give him. There were times when it was difficult for the Clares to feed their children, and there was always illness in the family through lack of food and undernourishment. The wages of a farm labourer were very low, and the outbreak of war with France in 1793 meant a sharp increase in the price of bread which was to cause terrible want and misery for the poor. Even before that, their plight was a pitiful one. Much of rural England was being swallowed up by the Parliamentary Acts of Enclosure – the absorption of common land into private ownership in the interests of agricultural efficiency and progress. This deprived the labourer of the ground on which he might graze his animals and collect fuel and building materials.

A succession of bad harvests between 1792 and 1814 meant that yields were well below expectations, and fears of starvation were very real. Children grew up on a diet of thin gruel and turnips. The poor were made increasingly poorer, and the fight to avoid debt and destitution became harder. The ranks of those in need of Poor Law relief grew. The 'Speenhamland System', introduced by Berkshire magistrates in May 1795, had become widespread. This scheme was intended to fix and enforce a minimum wage in relation to the price of bread, but it developed into an iniquitous system. The poor received from the parish rates a certain sum each week to supplement their wages as the price of flour and bread rose. The farmers could only gain. They could raise prices and increase their profit, but did not have to worry about paying higher wages. This meant that the rich grew richer and the poor grew poorer.

The Clares certainly had their share of poverty and were to know the humiliation of being listed as paupers. Under such conditions it was extremely difficult to bring up a family. Frederick W. Martin, Clare's first biographer, tells us that Parker and Ann Clare were 'among the poorest of the village, as their little cottage was among the narrowest and most wretched of the hundred mud hovels.'[2] But John himself recalled it as 'roomy and comfortable as any of our neighbours'.[3] Their landlord, Edward Gee, charged £2 a year rent and allowed them the use of a large garden, which Parker Clare used to dig early in the morning before he went to work, or at night when he came home. The vegetables that he grew there helped to augment the rather slender meals. There was also an apple tree in the garden, and its annual crop made enough money for them to pay the rent.

Gee, who was a retired farmer, lived in two rooms at the end of the cottage and was a good friend to his tenants. But when he died in August 1804 the new young farmer who took possession of the cottage divided it into four tenements, leaving the Clares with only one room downstairs and one bedroom, for which he charged them three guineas a year. What was once a comparatively spacious home was reduced to very cramped quarters. The garden was similarly divided into four strips, but as Parker Clare was the oldest tenant, he was allowed to choose that strip which had the apple tree. Fortunately its yield continued to make up the greater part of their rent.

At that time Parker Clare was an unusually strong man. He was popular at village feasts, and had something of a reputation as a wrestler. He also had a good voice and would boast that he could recite over a hundred ballads and sing as many songs – all learnt by heart, for he could read very little and write not at all.

Ann Clare doubtless had a store of these old ballads and songs in her memory, too, for singing and telling stories that had been handed down from generation to generation were popular pastimes. But she could neither read nor write, and 'superstition went so far with her that she believed the higher parts of learning was the blackest arts of witchcraft and that no other means could attain them.'[4] Her illiteracy was a source of great regret to her, and she determined to give her children as much education as possible. John later recalled: 'my mothers hopfull ambition ran high of being able to make me a good scholar, as she expirienced enough in her own case to avoid bringing up her childern in ignorance.'[5]

Books were scarce, and education was usually received at the knee of some old dame or under the stern eye of the village schoolmaster. And so, at the age of five, John was sent to the local dame school run by a Mrs Bullimore. Her teaching was elementary in the extreme; she had little to offer apart from the alphabet, some easy numbers and a few playground games. John learnt to write and to read a little from the Bible, but Mrs Bullimore's teaching did not make much impression upon him.

Because of their increasing poverty and the need to supplement the family income, John's parents were forced to send him out to work even earlier than was usual in rural areas at that time. When he was seven, he was taken away from Mrs Bullimore's school and sent out to tend the sheep and geese on Helpston Heath where he made friends with Mary Bains, commonly known as 'Granny Bains'. She was a local herdswoman and an accurate weather forecaster, and, as such, was respected by the villagers. But the thing that delighted John was her retentive memory in which was stored strange stories, songs, gossip and folklore which filled his mind with fantasies.

When he was about ten his father made him a small flail and took him threshing, an occupation for which he had little liking but which then became his usual work in winter. Looking back on those days he later recalled:

> Winter was generally my season of imprisonment in the dusty barn Spring and Summer my assistance was wanted elsewhere in tending sheep or horses in the fields or scaring birds from the grain or weeding it, which was a delightful employment, as the old womens memorys never failed of tales to smoothen our labour, for as every day came new Jiants, Hobgoblins, and faireys was ready to pass it away[6]

John was small for his age, but he worked well and did not flinch from the roughest labour, thereby gaining the approval of his masters who dubbed him 'weak but willing'. During the winter, when there was little work in the fields, from about the age of eight he attended a school held in the vestry at Glinton church, just over two miles away. Here he was taught by John Seaton, and later by James Merrishaw. The young student soon acquired a real hunger for knowledge, and worked hard day and night to perfect himself, not only in reading and writing, but also in algebra and arithmetic. At home, after the evening meal, the bare table was spread with books, pens, ink and paper. His mother watched with affection. Looking up from her spinning-wheel she more than once expressed her hope that one day he would reward them for all the trouble they had taken over his education.

John's desire to improve his knowledge continued undiminished. Sometimes he amused himself by writing on the whitewashed walls of barns or tracing his arithmetical symbols on the dusty floors. He improved his skills at every opportunity and, whatever the subject, learning became an obsession that was to stay with him for the rest of his life. He had, he tells us, 'a restless curiosity that was ever on the enquirey and never satisfied and when I got set fast with one thing I did not tire but tryed at another tho with the same success in the end yet it never sickened me I still pursued Knowledge in a new path.'[7]

Although John never mastered orthodox spelling or punctuation, the fact that someone in his class could write at all was unusual at a time when such accomplishment was discouraged. There was strong pressure against him developing his education, especially when there was the need to contribute to the family income. It was common in the village 'to pass judgement on a lover of books as a sure indication of laziness',[8] so he was driven 'to the narrow necessity of stinted oppertunitys to hide in woods and dingles of thorns in the fields on Sundays to read these things'[9]

Although Clare's early years were lived against constant struggle and want, the quality that emerges from his own account of childhood is one of almost visionary happiness. His pastimes were those of the other village children. He fished with a thread and a bent pin, fed on nuts and blackberries, and peas stolen from the fields, ran races and delighted in all the games of childhood. But at other times, when he was not playing games or fishing, he was beginning to develop a taste for solitude, and would often separate himself from his companions and walk alone for miles, studying the behaviour of birds, looking for wild flowers, or collecting snail shells. These lonely wanderings developed in him a passion for nature and all the creatures of the earth that was to bring him much pleasure and yet also to cause him much suffering. Looking back on those days he wrote:

> most of my sundays [were] spent in ... fields with such merry company I heard the black and the brown beetle sing their evening songs with rapture and lovd to see the black snail steal out upon its dewy baulks I saw the humble horse bee at noon 'spiring' on wanton wing I lovd to meet the woodman whistling away to his toils and to see the shepherd bending oer his hook on the thistly green chatting love storys to the listening maiden while she milkd her brindld cow the first primrose in spring was as delightful as it is now the copper colourd clouds of the morning was watched[10]

In his autobiographical notes written in the 1820s he describes an occasion when, as a very small boy, he wandered miles from home on an expedition in search of 'the world's end':

> I eagerly wandered on & rambled along the furse the whole day till I got out of my knowledge when the very wild flowers seemd to forget me & I imagind they were inhabitants of new countrys the very sun seemd to be a new one & shining in a different quarter in the sky[11]

John became so absorbed in the surrounding countryside that he arrived home late at night to find his parents distraught and half the village out searching for him. According to Frederick Martin, John had to endure 'a severe punishment for his romantic excursion'; the young wanderer 'did not mind the beating; but a long while after felt sad and sore at heart to have been unable to find the hoped-for country where heaven met earth.'[12]

It was not long before his strange behaviour marked him out from among the other boys of the village. He was, says Edward Storey, 'a dreamy boy who preferred his own company and had a habit of talking to himself.'[13] Nevertheless, friendship was an important factor in his childhood. One of his close friends was Richard Turnill, who was the younger son of a wealthy farmer. Richard was a quiet, refined boy, who was about John's age. They shared interests, exchanged books and played together. Ann Clare was happy to think that her son had found someone of his own age and no longer wanted to spend all his time alone. He records the relationship thus:

> Among all the friendships I have made in life those of school friendship and childish acquaintance are the sweetest to remember there is no deseption among them there is nothing of regret in them but loss they are the fairest and sunniest pages memory ever doubles down in the checkerd volume of life to refer to there is no blotches

upon them – they are not found like bargains on matters of interest nor broken for selfish ends ... what numberless hopes of successes did we chatter over as we hunted among the short snubby bushes of the heath or on hedge rows and crept among the black thorn spreys after the nest of the nightingales and what happy discourses of planning pleasures did we talk over as we lay on the soft summer grass gazing on the blue sky shaping the passing clouds to things familiar with our memorys and dreaming of the days to come when we should mix with the world and be men[14]

Richard Turnill died of typhus fever while still at school. Although Clare was deeply affected by his death, there began another friendship about this time which was destined to have a far greater influence on him. During his schooldays at Glinton he formed a passionate attachment to Mary Joyce, who was the daughter of James Joyce, a wealthy farmer. Born in January 1797, Mary was four years younger than Clare. This is how he described his relationship with her:

I was a lover very early in life my first attachment being a school boy affection but Mary – who cost me more ballads [than] sighs was belovd with a romantic or platonic sort of feeling if I could but gaze on her face or fancy a smile on her co[u]ntenance it was sufficient I went away satisfied we playd with each other but named nothing of love yet I fancyd her eyes told me her affections we walkd together as school companions in leisure hours but our talk was of play and our actions the wanton innocence of childern yet young as my heart was it would turn chill

> when I touchd her hand and trembled and I fancyd her feelings were the same for as I gazd earnestly in her face a tear would hang in her smiling eye and she would turn to wipe it away her heart was as tender as a birds[15]

They remained friends until 1816, when unexpectedly they separated. Frederick Martin has stated that the reason for their parting was that Mary's father objected to the relationship and forbade his daughter to see 'the beggar-boy' again.[16] But there was no evidence for this idea. It was Mary herself who realized the hopelessness of such a match. No doubt they met again when they were older, but Clare was evidently too sensitive about his poverty to make any attempt to overcome her resistance. He finished his account of their friendship with these comments:

> when she grew up to womanhood she felt her station above mine at least I felt that she thought so for her parents were farmers and Farmers had great pretentions to somthing then ... I felt the [disparity] in our situations and fearing to meet a denial I carried it on in my own fancies to every extreme writing songs to her praise and making her mine with every indulgence of the fancy[17]

Clare had hoped that one day he would be her equal, and that his dream of marrying her would become a reality. Although 'thwarted', his love for Mary lasted all his life and remained supreme through many other loves, and through all the years of married life; but there is no further trace of Mary Joyce, except for the record of her death, unmarried, in 1838.

NOTES

1. *John Clare by Himself*, edited by Eric Robinson and David Powell
2. Frederick W. Martin: *The Life of John Clare* (2nd edition, edited by Eric Robinson and Geoffrey Summerfield, 1964), page 2
3. *John Clare by Himself*, page 116
4. *Ibid.* page 3
5. *Ibid.*
6. *Ibid.* page 4
7. *Ibid.* page 59
8. *Ibid.* page 6
9. *Ibid.*
10. *Ibid.* pages 38-39
11. *Ibid.* pages 40-41
12. Frederick Martin: *The Life of John Clare*, page 7
13. Edward Storey: *The Right to Song*, page 46
14. *John Clare by Himself*, page 49
15. *Ibid.*
16. Frederick Martin: *The Life of John Clare*, page 22
17. *John Clare by Himself*, pages 87-88

CHAPTER 2

Seeking Employment

When he was twelve, with his schooldays now over, Clare's parents tried to find a suitable job for him. It was no easy matter. There was little work around Helpston that could make use of his education. A local shoemaker offered to take him as an apprentice, but he did not like the idea of cobbling. George Shelton, a stonemason, offered to take him, but this was no more to his taste than cobbling, and he said, by way of excuse, that he did not like climbing and had no head for heights – conveniently forgetting that he often climbed trees in search of birds' nests.

Parker and Ann Clare were almost in despair and began to think that their son was lazy. 'But the fact was,' John later wrote, 'I felt timid and fearful of undertaking the first trial in every thing.'[1] He did not want to leave home nor to work in any trade that was new to him. It was customary then for apprentices to live in with their employer, and the prospect of taking a job away from home filled Clare with dread. He later recalled:

> I felt a sort of hopeless prospect around me of not being able to meet manhood as I coud wish for I had always that feeling of ambition about me that wishes to do something to gain notice or to rise above its fellows[2]

Although his parents were naturally disappointed, they were determined not to commit John to a trade he would not enjoy. So he stayed on at home and worked in the fields, doing any odd jobs that came his way.

Eventually he was offered employment by Mrs Bellairs at Woodcroft Castle, two miles from Helpston, and he began to work there as a ploughboy. It was a good job and Mrs Bellairs was very kind to him, but he was not happy there and would not settle down. He objected to getting up early in the morning and to working in wet conditions. In wet weather the moat used to flow over the causeway that led to the porch. This meant that Clare had to wade up to his knees in icy water to get in and out. After only a few weeks he decided that he had had enough; nothing his parents could say would persuade him to return.

Very soon another opportunity occurred that filled the anxious parents with hopes of finding their son some work that would be more congenial to him and would offer him good prospects. Ann Clare's brother, Morris Stimson, worked for James Bellamy, a Wisbech lawyer and counsellor. There was a vacancy in Bellamy's office for a clerk, and Morris promised to do his best to get the boy a place. Counsellor Bellamy wished to see him in order to form an opinion of his character and qualifications.

To get there, Clare had to make the journey to Peterborough and then by boat along the River Nene to Wisbech twenty-one miles away. The boat only went once a week, leaving Peterborough on Friday and returning on Sunday. He set off for Wisbech, he tells us, 'with a timid sort of pleasure.'[3] It was 'a foreign land' to him, for he had never been above eight miles from home in his life, and he could not imagine England much larger than the part he knew.

Clare spent most of the journey thinking up answers to imaginary questions rather than observing the flat countryside through which he travelled.

> I put questions to myself and shaped proper replies as though I would succeed and then my heart burnt within me at the hopes of success and thoughts of the figure I should make afterwards when I went home to see my friends dressd up as a writer in a law[y]ers office[4]

A few hours later the barge tied up at the town bridge in Wisbech and the passengers disembarked. As soon as he stood on the quay Clare realised that he had been so preoccupied in rehearsing his interview that he had completely forgotten his uncle's directions to Mr Bellamy's house. It meant asking strangers the way. They stared at him with disbelief, wondering what this wide-eyed youth was doing away from home. By the time he found the house all his eloquent replies had evaporated. He rang the bell and was relieved when his uncle, the footman, opened the door and led him to the kitchen. Some food had been prepared for him, but he could eat nothing as he was anxiously trying to retrieve some of the thoughts he had planned on the barge, and wondering how he should manage to obey his uncle's instructions to 'look up boldly and tell him what you can do.'[5]

The interview, when it came, was brief, and Clare described it with a sense of humour:

> at length the counsellor appeared and I held my head as well as I coud but it was like my hat almost under my arm 'Aye aye so this is your Nephew Morris is he' said the couns[e]llor 'Yes Sir' said my uncle 'Aye aye so this is

> your Nephew' repeated the counsellor rubbing his hands as he left the room 'well I shall see him agen' – but he never saw me agen to this day[6]

Mrs Bellamy offered him bed and food in the servants' quarters until the boat returned to Peterborough on Sunday morning. He spent a whole day exploring Wisbech and amusing himself by looking at shop windows, in one of which he saw some paintings by Edward Rippingille, a self-taught artist from King's Lynn.

On Sunday morning the narrow boat returned to Peterborough and Clare had plenty of time to reflect on his failure to impress Mr Bellamy. His own disappointment was soon forgotten in his delight at seeing his beloved Helpston; but to his parents this latest failure of their son was a more serious matter, and they may well have wondered whether he would ever get steady work.

Fortunately their neighbour, Francis Gregory, who was the landlord of the Blue Bell Inn next door to the Clares, came to the rescue. He wanted a day-labourer, someone to do odd jobs and run errands. He agreed to take Clare for a year, and promised that he should have sufficient time of his own to continue his studies. Clare later recalled that 'it was a good place ... they treated me more like a son than a servant ... I believe I may say that this place was the nursery for my ryhmes'.[7]

One of his duties at the Blue Bell was to fetch a bag of flour once a week from the mill at Maxey, a village two miles from Helpston. He was, he tells us, 'of a very timid disposition':

> the traditional Registers of the Village was uncommonly superstitious ... and I had two or three haunted Spots to

> pass … therefore I must in such extremitys seize the best remedy to keep such things out of my head as well as I coud, so on these journeys I muttered over tales of my own fancy and contriving them into ryhmes as well as my abilities was able; … and tho however romantic my story might be I had cautions, fearful enough no doubt, to keep ghosts and hobgoblings out of the question … for as I passd those awful places, tho I dare not look boldly up, my eye was warily on the watch, glegging under my hat at every stir of a leaf or murmur of the wind and a quaking thistle was able to make me swoon with terror[8]

Clare worked hard for Gregory for a year, but he was no nearer full time employment than he had been a year ago. This is how he recorded matters:

> I … left with the restless hope of being something better than a plough boy … my little ambitions kept burning about me every now and then to make a better figure in the world and I knew not what to be at   A bragging fellow name[d] Manton from Market Deeping usd to frequent the public house when I livd there   he was a stone cutter and sign painter   he usd to pretend to discover something in me as deserving encouragement and wanted to take me apprentice to learn the misterys of his art but then he wanted the trifle with me that had disappointed my former posperitys   he usd to talk of his abilitys in sculpture and painting over his beer till I was almost mad with anxiety to be a sign painter and stone cutter but it was useless such things made my mind restless[9]

There soon came another opportunity for employment – this time as an apprentice to the kitchen gardener at Burghley House, near Stamford. When he heard of the vacancy, Clare, encouraged by his father, lost no time in applying. He was given the job and started work immediately. It was a three-year contract; but he was not happy there and left towards the end of his first year.

> I learnt irregular habits at this place which I had been a stranger to had I kept at home tho we was far from a town yet confinement sweetens liberty and we stole every opportunity to get to Stamford on summer evenings when I had no money to spend my elder companions would offer to treat me for the sake of my company there and back agen and to keep me from divulging the secret to my master by making me a partner in their midnight revels we usd to get out of the window and over the high wall of the extensive gardens for we slept in the garden house and was locked in every night to keep us from robbing the fruit I expect – Our place of rendevouse was a public house called 'the Hole in the wall', famous for strong ale and midnight merriment[10]

The drinking and singing went on until the early hours of the morning. Some of Clare's companions then went on to a local brothel and the others made their unsteady way home. When the head gardener realised that Clare had been involved in these escapades he threatened to dismiss him. Rather than have this happen, Clare decided to dismiss himself, and after another rowdy night in Stamford he persuaded his friend George Cousins that the time had come for them to leave Burghley and seek employment elsewhere.

So they got up early one morning in the autumn and walked to Grantham, twenty-one miles away. Clare felt as though they were in another world. They spent the night at The Crown and Anchor; the spirit of adventure grew faint in him and he wished himself at home, but he had gone too far now to turn back.

The following morning they set off for Newark-on-Trent, fifteen miles further north. After making many enquiries in the town, they eventually found work with Mr Withers, a local nurseryman, but Clare was very weak and found the long hours of work too heavy both for his strength and liking. Both men grew restless and unhappy. Once again they decided to look for something better and left by the first light of morning.

They were now depressed, and wondered if their adventure was such a good idea after all. On the way home they decided to spend their last few pence on drink and forget their troubles. Clare became so drunk that he made up his mind, though only seventeen, to offer himself for service in the Nottinghamshire Militia. Fortunately for him the recruiting officer did not think he was tall enough, and therefore rejected him.

The need to find work once more became a priority. Parker and Ann Clare were now heavily in debt. In the spring of 1811 John was nearly eighteen, but economic problems had deepened and there was now far less chance of work for him than there had been before. And so, in face of the threat of invasion by Napoleon, he decided again there was nothing else for him to do but offer himself for the Militia, this time in his own county. And so he walked to Oundle and enlisted in the Eastern Regiment of the Northamptonshire Militia, a reserve force behind the regular army.

The enlistment was for four years, and service involved training. During one training session Clare seized a bullying corporal by the throat and hurled him to the ground. Perhaps, in his anger, he had a sudden burst of strength! He was threatened with a few days in the 'Black Hole', but his captain came to his aid, heard his account of the incident as well as the corporal's, and punished the young recruit with just one extra guard duty. Clare had been let off lightly. Later he accepted two guineas to enlist for overseas duty, should he ever be needed – five shillings on signing the contract, and the rest when the time for call-up came. But he was not required; soon after the peace declaration of May 1814, the Northamptonshire Militia was disbanded, and Clare returned to live with his parents at Helpston.

The exact details of Clare's employment in the next two or three years are not known, but he worked sometimes in the fields and sometimes in the gardens of the local farmers. He would often spend his nights drinking, and sometimes – because he was too drunk to get home – had to sleep in a field. There were among his friends two brothers, John and James Billings, whose dilapidated old cottage formed a meeting place for the young men of the village. It was known as 'Bachelors Hall', and its reputation among the more respectable neighbours was not a very good one. The meetings, which took place every evening, were accompanied by heavy drinking and rowdy singing.

Some of the young men were guilty of poaching. They regarded it as a pleasant excitement and a source of considerable gain, and the money they freely acquired was often spent on drink. Though invited to accompany the Billings brothers on their expeditions to the woods, Clare would not join in the stealing of game; he loved all creatures and could not hurt or destroy even the least of them. But although unwilling to take part in poaching himself, he was prepared to share in its fruits, and it was not long before he became the leader at the frequent drinking bouts at Bachelors Hall. Shy and reserved on ordinary occasions, he was at these meetings the loudest of them all with his talking and singing.

About this time Clare associated himself with the gypsies, who were often to be found camping on Helpston Heath. He was fascinated by their dark eyes and strange talk. He was accepted by the Smiths and Boswells as a friend who was always welcome, and he often shared their evening meal with them. He used to spend his Sundays and summer evenings among them, 'learning to play the fiddle in their manner by the ear and joining in their pastimes of jumping dancing and other amusements.'[11]

From what Clare tells us, it seems that he had a number of light-hearted flirtations at this time, probably with one or two gypsies as well as the local girls. The only one that we know about was quite a serious affair and lasted, on and off, for some time. This was with Elizabeth Newbon who lived in the nearby village of Ashton. It seems that Clare had forgotten so much about his friendship with Mary Joyce that he refers to Elizabeth as 'my first love'[12] who, though not apparently blessed with good looks, appeared very attractive to John who 'fancyd she was everything.'[13] Her father was a wheelwright and a keen student of the Bible. As the courtship progressed, Clare was allowed to meet Elizabeth at her home, where Mr Newbon used to question him to test his knowledge of the scriptures. 'My silence,' Clare wrote, 'generally spoke my lack of religion and he shook his head at my ignorance.'[14] Finally, after 'petty jealousies on both sides', Elizabeth accused him of 'changing affections'[15] and they parted, which does not seem to have worried Clare unduly.

Parker Clare was now so crippled with rheumatism that he could hardly stand. When he did walk it was with the aid of two sticks. But his spirit was, as his son said of him, 'strongly knitted with independence and the thoughts of being forced to bend before the frowns of a Parish to him was the greatest despair, so he stubbornly strove with his infirmitys and potterd about the roads putting stones in the ruts for his 5 shillings a week, fancying he was not so much beholden to their forced generosity as if he had taken it for nothing I myself was of a weak const[i]tution and a severe indisposition keeping me from work for a twelvemonth ran us in debt we had back rents to make up, some bills, and Bakers etc etc ... my fathers assistance was now disabled and the whole weight fell upon myself, who at the best of times was little capable to bear it.'[16]

Clare's 'severe indisposition' seems to have been the recurrence of a fainting fit brought about by his witness of a fatal farm accident when he was a child. But, indisposed or not, he had to earn enough money to keep his parents out of the workhouse. So, with no chance of getting a job in Helpston, he set out, in the spring of 1817, with Stephen Gordon to become a lime burner at Bridge Casterton, north of Stamford. Their employer was a Mr Wilders who owned several kilns in the area, and who expected his men to work long hours:

> we worked at first from light to dark (and in some emergencys all night) to get some money to appear a little descent in a strange place having arivd pennyless with a shabby appearance ... in the bargain we got lodgings at a house of scant fame a professd lodging house kept by a man and his wife of the name of Cole and we was troubled at night with [three] in each bed an inconvenience which I had never been usd to they took in men of all descriptions the more the merrier for their profits and when they all assembled round the evening fire the

> motly co[u]ntenances of many characters lookd like an assembledge of robbers in the rude hut dimly and my[s]teriously lighted by the domestic savings of a farthing taper …
>
> … When we first went we workd hard to save money and tryd to be saving in which we succeeded for a time as I got about 50 shillings in about 6 weeks with which I intended to purchase a new olive green coat a color which I had long aimd at and for which I was measured already ere I left home expecting to be able to pay for it in a short time but an accident happened in the way which prevented me[17]

Exactly what that accident was we do not know. He may have been referring to some trouble after a drinking bout, or maybe some pressure from a creditor or some kind of blackmail. Whatever it was, it cost him his olive green coat.

Clare's employer, who was landlord of the New Inn at Casterton, had a kiln in that village, another in the neighbouring village of Ryhall, and was about to open a third at Pickworth, some four miles away. But when he heard that Clare had worked in the gardens of Burghley House, he offered him work in his own garden at the New Inn. So Clare left the lime kiln for a season in the garden. In the summer he went, with Stephen Gordon, to burn lime at the Pickworth kiln. The village of Pickworth he calls 'a place of other days', and adds that the piece of ground where they 'dug the kiln was full of … human bones.'[18]

On Sundays Clare and his companions went for long walks, usually ending up in the village of Tickencote where there was a public house called the Flower Pot. It was on one of his visits to the Flower Pot that he first saw Martha Turner as she made her way across the fields to Walkherd Lodge, between Casterton and Pickworth. He tells us that though 'in love at first sight', he did not know which way she was going. 'But,' he records, 'chance quickly threw her again in my way a few weeks after one evening when I was going to [play the] fiddle at Stamford ... I then venturd to speak to her and succeeded so far as [to] have the liberty to go home with her to her cottage about 4 miles off and it became the introduction to some of the happiest and unhappiest days my life has met with.'[19]

Martha Turner was born on 3rd March 1799. When she met Clare she was, according to Frederick Martin, 'a fair girl of eighteen, slender, with regular features, and pretty blue eyes.'[20] Clare took to calling her 'Patty' about a year after their first meeting. She was the daughter of a cottage farmer, and seems to have welcomed Clare's courtship from the beginning. There was, however, considerable opposition from her parents who considered a lime burner a very unfitting match for their daughter. A shoe maker from Stamford was courting her at the same time, and as he had his own shop and every prospect of getting on in the world, they considered him to be a much more desirable match and tried their hardest to persuade her to agree. But Patty knew her own mind and would have none of her parents' advice.

Towards the end of the year, Clare's employer reduced his wages to seven shillings a week; but he believed he could earn that amount in Helpston, so he handed in his notice and returned to live with his parents. But work was not easy to find, and he returned to his old habits of late night drinking sessions with his friends. For a time he even lost interest in Patty. With his hopes of success shattered he took refuge from his troubles in an affair with Betty Sell who lived at Southorpe, near the village of Barnack. He met Betty at Stamford Fair and went out with her several times during the next few months, but it only added to his troubles, for he tells us that the affair 'grew up in to an affection that made my heart ache to think it must be broken.' Patty was pregnant by him and 'in a situation that only marriage could remedy'.[21]

Clare was in a dilemma. He was torn between his duty to one girl and his affection for the other, and had no particular wish to marry either of them, for responsibilities already lay upon his shoulders.

> I felt awkwardly situated and knew not which way to proceed   I had a variety of minds about me and all of them unsettld   my long smotherd affections for Mary revivd with my hopes and as I expected to be on a level with her bye and bye I thought then I might have a chance of success in renewing my former affections ... amid these delays Pattys emergencys became urgent   she had reveald her situation to her parents when she was unable to conseal it any longer who upbraided her with not heeding their advice and told her as she had made her bed hard she should lye on it ... when I reflected on these things I felt stubbornly disposd to leave them the risk of her misfortunes but when she complained of their [coldness towards her] I could stand out no longer and promisd that my prosper[i]ty should make me her friend and to prove that I was in earnest I gave her money to [bolster her] independence till we should be married   this behaviour pacified them and left her at peace[22]

NOTES

1. *John Clare by Himself,* page 67
2. *Ibid.* page 68
3. *Ibid.* page 67
4. *Ibid.* page 70
5. *Ibid.* page 71
6. *Ibid.*
7. *Ibid.* page 66
8. *Ibid.* page 9
9. *Ibid.* pages 66-67
10. *Ibid.* page 74
11. *Ibid.* page 83
12. *Ibid.* page 89
13. *Ibid.*
14. *Ibid.*
15. *Ibid.* page 88
16. *Ibid.* page 18
17. *Ibid.* pages 79-81
18. *Ibid.* page 92
19. *Ibid.* page 90
20. *The Life of John Clare,* page 54
21. *John Clare by Himself,* page 111
22. *Ibid.* page 112

CHAPTER 3

'A thinker from a boy'

During the months of unemployment Clare used to walk to Ashton Green, about a mile from Helpston, to see his friend Tom Porter. They had known each other since childhood. Porter was fond of gardening and collecting wild flowers, and he and Clare used to go out on Sundays to search for rare plants. Their tastes were parallel in everything except poetry. Porter was, nevertheless, a lover of books and Clare borrowed the few books that he possessed. Looking back on those days Clare wrote:

> conjectures filld the village about my future destinations on the stage of life, some fancying it symptons of lunacy and that my mothers prophecys would be verified to her sorrow and that my reading of books (they would jeeringly say) was for no other improvement than qualifying an idiot for the workhouse, for at this time my taste and passion for reading began to be furious and I never strolled out on a Sabbath day but some scrap or other was pocketed for my amusement[1]

From his autobiographical notes and sketches it would appear that much of Clare's early life, and the bulk of his early reading material, centred on the chapbooks and broadsides. Chapbooks were literally cheap books, often sold uncut and unstitched in the form of a single sheet to be cut and bound by the purchaser. They often contained fairy tales, ballads and old folk tales. A broadside was a single sheet printed on one side only. It usually contained the text of a song, sometimes of a narrative or dialogue. Frequently illustrated, by means of either a woodblock or a steel engraving, these were sold generally for a penny by hawkers and ballad sellers.

Clare recalled: 'The first books I got hold of beside the bible and prayer book was an old book of Essays with no title and then a large one on Farming Robin Hoods Garland and the Scotch Rogue,'[2] though from his writings it would appear that these chapbooks and others had already become part of the Clare household. John writes of his father reading them to him:

> what first induced me to ryhme I cannot hardly say the first thing that I heard of poetry that may be called poetry was a romantic story, which I have since found to be Pomfret's 'Love triumphant over reason' by reading of it over since to my father who remembered the Story, but I could benefit little by this as I used to hear it before I could read and my father was but a sorry reader of poetry to improve his readers by reciting it ... the relating any thing under the character of a dream is a captivating way of drawing the attention of the vulgar and to my knowledge tale or vision as it is called of Pomfrets is more known among the lower orders than any thing else of poetry at least with us[3]

The presence of such chapbooks in the house and in the possession of his friends sparked an interest in the young John Clare, who saved hard to buy more of them.

> I had always that feeling of ambition about me that wishes to do something to gain notice or to rise above its fellows ... I was fond of books before I began to write poetry these were such that chance came at – 6py Pamphlets that are in the possession of every door calling hawker and found on every book stall at fairs and markets whose titles are as familiar with every one as his own name ... 'Little red riding hood' 'Valentine and Orson' 'Jack and the Jiant' 'Tom Long the carrier' 'The king and the cobler', 'Sawney Bean' 'The seven Sleepers' 'Tom Hickathrift' 'Idle Laurance' who carried that power spell about him that laid every body to sleep – 'old mother Bunch' 'Robin Hoods garland' 'old mother Shipton and old Nixons Prophecys' 'History of Gotham' and many others ... these have memorys as common as Prayer books and Psalters with the peasantry such were the books that delighted me and I savd all the pence I got to buy them for they were the whole world of literature to me and I knew no other I carried them in my pocket and read them at my leisure and they was the never weary food of winter evenings ere Milton Shakespeare and Thomson had [an] existence in my memory and I even feel a love for them still ... I know I am foolish enough to have fancys different from others ... but I ... cannot help it[4]

Clare's first attempts at poetry were, he recalls, 'imitations of my fathers Songs'.[5] Even before he could read, John was introduced to an oral culture that was largely couched in rhyme. From the songs that his father sang he would have become aware of rhyme, rhythm, verse structure and narrative. Once he had acquired a rudimentary reading skill, his library was principally composed of chapbooks and broadsides. It was not until he attended school at Glinton that he became aware of more lofty literary works, but according to George Deacon, 'by this time he had already been exposed to a self-entertainment culture which had at its root a rhyming rhythmic musicality which must have insinuated itself into his mind.'[6] John Clare the poet was partly a product of his own culture and society, where poetry and song were normal rather than extraordinary forms.

When Clare was thirteen, a young friend lent him a battered copy of James Thomson's *The Seasons*, so battered in fact that most of 'Winter' was missing. His friend had become a Methodist and now, he told Clare, he preferred Wesley's hymns. All the same, the book was such a precious possession he did not *give* it to Clare. So, having persuaded his father to give him eighteen pence, young John walked to Stamford to buy a copy, only to find the shop closed because it was Sunday. So he walked all the way there again early next morning and purchased it. Published in 1730, *The Seasons* was the first major nature poem in English and a forerunner of the Romantic movement. Thomson challenged the artificiality of the fashionable poetry of his day, and inaugurated a new era through his sentiment for nature. A master of description, he also wrote as a 'philosopher', concerned with the effect of the seasons on various parts of nature, ascending from the lower to the higher.

Clare could not bear to wait until he got home to read it, so he climbed over the wall into Burghley Park and there began with 'Spring'. These are the lines which made his heart 'twitter with joy':

> Come, gentle Spring, ethereal mildness, come,
> And from the bosom of yon dropping cloud,

While music wakes around, veil'd in a shower
Of shadowing roses, on our plains descend ...

As he continued his journey homewards, he 'got into a strain of descriptive ryhming' which resulted in his composing 'The Morning Walk', 'the first thing [he] committed to paper'.[7] He recalls the occasion in his autobiographical *Sketches*:

> I now venturd to commit my musings readily to paper but with all secressy possible, hiding them when written in an old unused cuppard in the chamber which when taken for other purposes drove me to the necessity of seeking another safety in a hole under the wall here my mother when clearing the chamber found me out and secretly took my papers for her own as occasion calld for them and as I had no other desire in me but to keep them from being read when laid in this fancied repository, that desire seemd compleated and I rarely turnd to a reperusal of them consequently my stolen fugitives went a long time ere they was miss'd my mother thought they was nothing more than Copies as attempts of improving my self in writing she knew nothing of poetry, at least little dreamed her son was employed in that business, and I was ashamed of being found out as an attempter in that way, when I discovered her thefts I humourd her mistake a long time and said they was nothing more than what she supposed them to be so she might take them but when I did things that I liked better than others I provided safer lodgings for them[8]

From then on, he tells us, 'poetry was a troublesome but pleasant companion anoying and cheering me at my toils.'[9] As a gardener in the village, he says, 'I could not stop my thoughts and often faild to keep them till night so when I fancyd I had hit upon a good image or natural description I usd to steal into a corner of the garden and clap it down but the appearance of my employers often put my fancys to flight.'[10] He found working in the fields easier in this respect: 'I usd to drop down behind a hedge bush or dyke and write down my things upon the crown of my hat.'[11] Most of his writing, however, seems to have been accomplished on Sundays, when he forsook the 'church going bell' to pursue instead 'the religion of the fields' and 'the restless revels of ryhme'.[12]

After a time, Clare began to long for a little encouragement and, without wholly divulging what he was about, to seek the opinion of his parents. He would read his poems aloud, and pretend that what he was reading was 'out of a borrowd book and that it was not my own.' He records that he 'scribbled on unceasing for 2 or 3 years, reciting [his poems] every night as I wrote them when my father returnd home from labour and we was all seated by the fire side.'[13] His parents were his first critics, and he claims to have found their criticism 'helpful' because 'I thought if they could not understand me my taste should be wrong founded and not agreable to nature, so I always ... wrote my pieces according to their criticisms, little thinking when they heard me read them that I was the author.'[14] His only confidant in this matter was Tom Porter, who seemed unimpressed by the verses, though he certainly kept the secret.

Clare continued to write, and as he built up a body of work, he decided to reveal his secret to his parents. He also cautiously approached people outside the family for their comments, but it seemed to the young poet that everyone was against him. The villagers laughed at him, and his parents, kind and sympathetic though they were, were convinced that his literary efforts were a waste of time and would, if not checked, keep him from getting an honest living. Clare's faith in himself burned so low that he questioned the use of going on. He began to write less and spend much of his leisure time drinking with the wildest characters of the village.

Despite all this discouragement, he had that vision which left him 'itching after rhyme', and in the summer of 1814 he decided that it was time to start preserving the best of his poems in a book, ready for that day when someone might show an interest. He knew exactly what he wanted – a stoutly bound volume of blank pages with a special title page. One day he walked to Market Deeping and tried to buy one from the printer and bookseller, J.B. Henson. Puzzled as to why the untidy-looking labourer should want such a book, Henson said that he had nothing like it in stock but he could make one up for about eight shillings. That was about a week's wages, but Clare would not let that hamper his dreams.

Henson promised to bind one up for him, but he was evidently filled with curiosity to know what a young labourer was going to do with a manuscript book. Clare tells us that 'being at that time released from my timid embarasment of reserve from a free application of Ale at the fair, I bluntly told him my intentions and as he was a printer of that extent of business in having types sufficient to enable him to print a pamphlet or small book now and then when he could happen of employment he doubtless fancyd I was a bargain, so he wishd to see some of my poems.'[15]

Early in 1817 he gave Henson a group of poems which included the sonnets 'The Setting Sun' and 'To a Primrose'. Henson was sufficiently impressed to offer Clare the hope of getting some of the work published. The best way to bring this about was to issue a printed prospectus, display it in bookshops or hawk it from door to door, and collect subscriptions sufficient to justify the cost of printing. The idea was not at all to Clare's liking, for he felt that it would be 'little better than begging money from people that knew nothing of their purchase',[16] and the thoughts of the jeers that he would meet when he issued his prospectus was more than enough to check his ambition for a time; but realising that there was no other way in which he could hope to get his poems published, he finally decided to brave the ridicule and go ahead.

Henson agreed to print three hundred copies of a prospectus for one pound, and promised that as soon as one hundred subscribers had given in their names he would begin to print the book at his own expense; but he indicated that Clare must compose the prospectus himself. The task presented great difficulties to the poet who, although he was happy enough in writing verses, was ill at ease when he tried his hand at prose. Eventually, after several attempts, he accomplished the task. The title of the prospectus was: *Proposals for Publishing by Subscription, a Collection of Original Trifles, on miscellaneous Subjects, religious and moral, in Verse, by John Clare of Helpstone*. But the prospectus contained such modest, even negative phrases, that it was hardly likely to rouse its readers into rapturous support:

> The public are requested to observe that the Trifles humbly offered for their candid perusal can lay no claim to eloquence of composition (whoever thinks so will be deceived), the greater part of them being *Juvenile* productions ... It is hoped that the humble situation which distinguishes their author will be some excuse in their

> favour, and serve to make an atonement for the many inaccuracies and imperfections that will be found in them ... May they be allowed to live their little day, and give satisfaction to those who may choose to honour them with a perusal, they will gain the end for which they were designed, and their author's wishes will be gratified. Meeting with this encouragement, it will enduce him to publish a similar collection, of which this is offered as a specimen ...[17]

The 'specimen' was the sonnet 'The Setting Sun', one of his earliest. On receiving the prospectus, Henson, anxious to get the poems into print, produced three hundred copies within a week. He sent one hundred copies to Clare and invited him to meet him at the Dolphin Inn, Stamford, to consider the progress. But the first thing Clare discovered when he arrived at the appointed place was that Henson had increased the cost of printing by five shillings. 'This,' Clare wrote, 'led me into his principles of overreaching and encroaching and from that time I considered him in his true light as being no friend of mine further than interest directed him, which turned out exactly the case.'[18]

While Clare and Henson were talking together in the Dolphin, a man came in to whom Henson offered a copy of the prospectus, but, Clare records, 'the fellow just threw his eyes over it, then looked at me and walked out of the room without saying a word.'[19] His spirits were sadly dashed, but soon afterwards a clergyman came in who read the prospectus with interest, praised the sonnet, and invited Clare to drink with him. He also told Henson to put his name down as a subscriber, saying he felt sure the publication would be a success. The unexpected encouragement restored Clare's confidence. What pleased him most of all was that the stranger had been impressed, not so much by the poet's 'humble situation' as by the quality of his poetry. That first subscriber was the Reverend Thomas Mounsey, a master of the Stamford Free Grammar School, and for a while the hopes aroused by this first success seemed likely to be realised. Clare wrote to Henson:

> I send you some of the principal Subscribers which I have procured lately: the first of which is a Baronet!!! who speaks very highly of my 'Sonnet' in the prospectus – Good God, how great are my Expectations! what hopes do I cherish! ... Please do all in your power to procure Subscribers (as your address will be look'd on better than that of a Clown) when 100 is got you may print if you please so do your best – & if it ever lies in my power to give friendship its due you shall not go unrewarded[20]

But the hundred subscribers did not respond to the invitation. After three months only seven subscribers had been found, and only one of them had paid. Clare's eager hopes were soon shattered. Despite this set-back, he went on preparing poems for the proposed volume. But Henson now wanted an advance of £15 before he would begin printing. Such a sum was utterly impossible, for Clare had 'not 15 pence nor 15 farthings',[21] and there was, therefore, no alternative but to give up the idea of publishing his poems.

Soon Clare's lack of fifteen shillings involved him in a worse situation. He was much distressed to receive a bill for that amount from a Stamford bookseller called Thompson, who kept the New Public Library in the High Street, and from whom he had received several magazines and books. Thompson demanded immediate payment, as he was selling his business and leaving town. Clare wrote to say that he could not possibly pay that amount all at once, but would do so by instalments.

So he sent his friend Thomas Porter to Stamford, instructing him to deliver his note and pacify the bookseller; he also enclosed some copies of his prospectus and the names of a few subscribers. But Thompson was not interested and told Porter that he wanted his money and would take care that he got it. Fortunately for Clare the conversation was overheard by Edward Drury, who had just arrived in Stamford to take over Thompson's business. He was a descendent of the famous Elizabethan family in whose honour one of London's famous thoroughfares was named – Drury Lane. He was the son of John Drury, a Lincoln printer whose sister was mother of John Taylor, the London publisher.

Drury took a copy of Clare's prospectus and entered into conversation with Tom Porter and, after asking various questions, he paid Clare's debt, with a promise to enquire further about him. Drury was a keen businessman with a wise judgement in literary matters, and he saw that this chance encounter with the work of a young peasant poet might well be turned to his advantage.

Drury lost no time. A few days later, accompanied by Robert Newcomb, who was the proprietor of the *Stamford Mercury*, he visited Clare at his home in Helpston. Drury said little to Clare at their first meeting and left it to Newcomb to ask most of the questions. Newcomb wanted to know how many poems Clare had written, where they were, how they were to be published, and what agreement he had made with Henson.

When Clare told them, the two men expressed their surprise and said that they would pay him instead of demanding payment to print them. By the end of their visit both Drury and Newcomb felt that Clare was 'good property'. As they left the cottage Newcomb invited him to have lunch with him the following Monday, adding on reflection that the invitation stood only if he had manuscripts to deliver, otherwise he was not to come. Clare found these remarks almost offensive. Nevertheless, it was an opportunity he could not miss.

His next concern was to retrieve the poems he had sent to Henson, who by now became anxious to retain them, holding that Clare had incurred responsibility by agreeing to let him publish them. Clare replied that he considered the agreement broken by the request for £15, which he could not obtain, and asked Henson to return the manuscripts. This Henson did with some reluctance.

Clare wasted no time in taking his poems to Edward Drury, deliberately ignoring Newcomb's invitation to lunch. Drury was delighted to have the poems in his possession so soon. He gave the poet a guinea, and encouraged him to bring all the remaining poems he might have so that a suitable collection could be made.

Drury, before making any further move in the matter, decided to obtain an estimate of the literary value of Clare's poems, so he sent them to the Reverend Mr Twopenny of Little Casterton, who returned them with the comment that he saw no harm in raising Clare a small subscription, but felt that his poems, which were full of many blunders in grammar and spelling, appeared to possess no merit worthy of publication. Clare took this criticism to heart:

> I felt my fortune as lost and my hopes gone and tho [Drury] tryd to cheer me I felt degected a long time and almost carried it too far   after prosperity shone out upon me I rememberd it keenly and wrote the following lines on his

name and a letter which I never sent
Towpenny [sic] his wisdom is and towpenny his fame is
Towpenny his merit is and towpenny his name is
And as twopence is a trifle I well may do without him
Ill sing in spite of twopenny and not care twopence
about him[22]

Clare's spirits, so cruelly dashed by Mr Twopenny, were soon to rise again, because Drury found a more friendly critic in Sir John English Dolben of Northampton, who appreciated his poems and said he would gladly subscribe to their publication. Drury was sufficiently satisfied by this response to send the poems to his cousin, John Taylor, in London. Taylor, a talented author as well as bookseller, was already publishing the works of William Hazlitt, Charles Lamb, Thomas de Quincey, Henry Francis Cary and John Keats. At a glance Taylor saw the true poetic nature of John Clare. He saw that 'under an uncouth garb, there were nameless beauties in the verses submitted to him; a wealth of feeling, and a depth of imagination seldom found in poetic descriptions of the external aspects of nature.'[23]

Drury knew that, having gone this far for an opinion, he would have to accept whatever verdict his cousin gave. He had no intention of handing Clare over to Taylor without protecting his own interests, for he believed that there could be profit in these poems as much for himself as for anyone else; but he needed Taylor's support.

John Taylor, born in 1781 at Retford, was the son of a bookseller, James Taylor, who had married Elizabeth Drury at Newark in September 1778. He moved to London in 1803, and after working for some years, first for James Lackington, who ran the well known Temple of the Muses, and then for the firm of Verner and Hood, he formed a partnership with James Augustus Hessey to set up their own business in Fleet Street. By 1819 they had built up a sound and progressive business. Taylor held dinner parties to which he invited authors and their patrons.

Taylor was particularly interested in Clare's poetry and the circumstances in which it had been written. He soon realised that the story of the 'peasant' poet would be an excellent advertisement for the poems, and he did everything he could to ensure a favourable reception of Clare's first book. In this he found a useful ally in Octavius Gilchrist.

Gilchrist owned a grocery business in Stamford. In his leisure time he indulged his tastes for scholarship and literary criticism, and he became a recognised authority on Elizabethan drama, and in 1805 published a volume of poems and helped William Gifford edit the works of Ben Johnson. Gilchrist was a man of catholic tastes and lively humour, no shirker of controversy, whether political or literary. He was a kind and understanding person who, although fourteen years older, was to become one of Clare's closest friends and allies.

Back in London, Taylor saw that John Clare's poems were 'diamonds which wanted polishing'[24] and this labour he resolved to undertake. He informed Drury of his intention to publish the poems under his own editorship and supervision, telling him to encourage Clare to devote himself more and more to the study of style and grammar, as well as to the improvement of his general education. Drury passed this message on to Clare; but he also made it clear that the success of the publication, as of all books, could not be guaranteed; therefore he must not indulge in too many hopes of gaining either fame or fortune.

Back at home again in December 1819, Clare needed all his hopes for the success of the book, for his parents owed two years' rent and were faced with eviction. He became depressed and felt that his poetry had dried up in the bleakness of that winter. Even Drury became concerned and paid off all the arrears, and thereby made it possible for Clare and his parents to stay in their cottage for at least another year. He also gave Clare the freedom of his shop in Stamford, where he could read the latest books which arrived from London, or write more poems.

It was at Drury's shop that Clare was eventually to meet his publisher, who was staying with Octavius Gilchrist. Taylor told Clare that he had worked on editing his poems, that he had compiled a glossary of the dialect words he had retained, that he had placed advertisements in the press, and that his poems would be published in the New Year.

Poems Descriptive of Rural Life and Scenery by John Clare A Northamptonshire Peasant was published by Taylor and Hessey, and Edward Drury, on 16th January 1820, with an Introduction by Taylor in which he gave an outline of Clare's life and circumstances:

> The following poems will probably attract some notice by their intrinsic merit; but they are also entitled to attention from the circumstances under which they were written. They are the genuine productions of a young Peasant, a day-labourer in husbandry, who has had no advantages of education beyond others of his class; and though poets in this country have seldom been fortunate men, yet he is, perhaps, the least favoured by circumstances, and the most destitute of friends, of any that existed.[25]

Taylor goes on to develop this idea – that Clare's poetry is valuable because it is by a peasant, and because it is extraordinary that he has managed to scrape together enough learning to gain access to the value which resides in true poetry. Taylor was, of course, concerned to sell the volume, and he is here tapping into several public responses: he appealed that they should, in a sense, regard Clare as a worthy object of charity (the Introduction ends with an appeal that the poet's expectation of a 'better life' should not be disappointed). Taylor's main point is, that though Clare's poetry reflects penury and hardship which most poets (even struggling ones) cannot match, it is this experience that gives it an undeniable value:

> At his own home ... he saw Poverty in all its most affecting shapes, and when he speaks of it ... he utters 'no idly feign'd poetic pains': it is a picture of what he has constantly witnessed and felt. One of our poets has gained great credit by his delineations of what the poor man suffers; but in the reality of wretchedness, when the 'iron enters into the soul', there is a tone which cannot be imitated. Clare has here an unhappy advantage over other poets. The most miserable of them were not always wretched. Penury and disease were not constantly at their heels, nor was pauperism their only prospect. But he has no other, for the lot which has befallen his father, may, with too much reason, be looked forward to as the portion of his own old age.[26]

NOTES

1. *John Clare by Himself*, page 5
2. *Ibid*. page 57
3. *Ibid*. page 14
4. *Ibid*. pages 68-69

5. *Ibid.* page 98
6. George Deacon: *John Clare and the Folk Tradition,* page 75
7. *John Clare by Himself,* pages 10-11
8. *Ibid.* page 13
9. *Ibid.* page 77
10. *Ibid.*
11. *Ibid.* page 78
12. *Ibid.*
13. *Ibid.* page 14
14. *Ibid.*
15. *Ibid.* page 20
16. *Ibid.*
17. Mark Storey (ed.): *Clare: The Critical Heritage,* page 30
18. *John Clare by Himself,* page 23
19. *Ibid.* page 106
20. Mark Storey (ed.): *The Letters of John Clare* page 3
21. *John Clare by Himself,* page 24
22. *Ibid.* page 109
23. Frederick Martin: *The Life of John Clare,* page 81
24. *Ibid.*
25. Mark Storey (ed.): *Clare: The Critical Heritage,* page 43
26. *Ibid.* page 44

CHAPTER 4

'Wearing into the sunshine'

Poems Descriptive of Rural Life and Scenery proved to be enormously successful, and within a year it was well into its fourth edition. Clare received news of its success from the Reverend Isaiah Holland, a Congregational Minister at Market Deeping. He had given Clare much support and encouragement during his struggle to get his poems published. Holland had received a letter from London telling him of the impact the poems had made in the Capital, and he lost no time in telling the poet.

The critics were mostly enthusiastic. William Gifford in the *Quarterly Review* of May 1820 devoted nine pages to a description and praise of Clare's poems, speaking of them as 'the most interesting literary productions of the day'.[1] One of his poems, 'The Meeting', had been set to music by Haydn Corri and Madame Vestris sang it to a crowded audience at Drury Lane. The chief talk in London was about the verses of the Northamptonshire Peasant.

Honours came in fast upon Clare. He was, as he put it, 'wearing into the sunshine'.[2] Hardly a day went by without some visitors turning up in Helpston. This was a new era in Clare's life; he found himself suddenly whirled from a quiet backwater into a turbulent mid-stream. In the months that followed events crowded upon him, each one a strange and disturbing experience to a man accustomed to the obscurity of poverty and the solitude of his native fields.

In February 1820 Clare was invited to Milton Hall, a place he had visited in earlier days in very different circumstances. During the preparation of *Poems Descriptive* he had written to Lord Milton asking permission to dedicate the work to him, but his Lordship was just setting off for Italy and forgot to answer his letter. On the publication of his work, Clare asked his mother to deliver a copy to Milton Hall. She returned with the exciting news that Lord Milton had asked for ten more copies and an invitation for the poet to visit him the following Sunday. Edward Drury sent Clare one of his own shirts and advised him not to pay the visit in his Sunday clothes, 'which are more suitable to a Squire of high degree than humble John Clare.'[3] So Clare went to Milton Hall dressed as a farm labourer. He records his visit:

> on the following sunday I went and after sitting awhile in servants hall where I could eat and drink nothing for thought his Lordship sent for me and instantly explaind the reasons why he did not answer my letter in a quiet unaffected manner which set me at rest he told me he had heard of my poems by parson Mossop who I have since heard took hold of every oppertunity to speak against my success or poetical abilitys before the book was published and then when it came out and others praisd it instantly turnd round to my side
>
> Lady Milton also askd me several questions and wishd me to name any book that was a favourite expressing at the same time a desire to give me one but I was confounded and could think of nothing so I lost the present in fact I

> did not like to pick out a book for fear of seaming overreaching on her kindness or else Shakespear lay at my togues end Lord fitzwilliam and lady fitzwilliam too talked to me and noticed me kindly and his Lordship gave me some advice which I had done well perhaps to have noticed better [than] I have he bade me beware of book-sellers and warned me not to be fed with promises[4]

On his departure they gave Clare a handful of money, which he dared not look at until well away from the house. It was more than he had ever possessed in his life. He records: 'I almost felt that I should be poor no more there was seventeen pound.'[5] He could not make enough haste back to Helpston to show his parents.

A few days later Clare was invited by Henry Pierrepont to meet the Marquis of Exeter at Burghley House. He was to go on the following Sunday, and to take the manuscripts of his poems with him. But when the day came it began to snow 'too unmercifully for a traveller ever to venture thus far'.[6] So he declined to go, though he admitted it was not the weather which prevented him from making the journey but the fear that his shoes would get too dirty to be seen in such a fine place. When he did go, a day later, the porter asked him why he had not come when expected. Clare blamed the weather and was told, 'You should stand for no weather tho it rained knives & forks with the tynes downward.'[7] After a while the Marquis sent for him. This is how Clare records the occasion:

> I ... went upstairs and thro winding passages after the footman as fast as I could hobble almost fit to quarrel with my hard naild shoes at the noise they made on the marble

> and boarded floors and cursing them to myself as I set my feet down in the lightest steps I was able to utter his Lordship received me kindly askd me some questions and requested to look at the MSS which Mr Pierpont wishd me to bring in my pocket after I had been about half an hour eyeing the door and now and then looking at my dirty shoes and wishing myself out of the danger of soiling such grandeur he saw my embarassments as I suspect and said that I should loose my dinner in the servants hall and said that I had better go but it was no use starting for I was lost and could not stir a foot I told his Lordship and he kindly opened the door and showed me the way when he suddenly made a stop in one of the long passages and told me that he had no room in his gardens for work at present but that he would allow me 15 guineas a year for life[8]

Early in March 1820, at the invitation of his publisher, John Taylor, Clare made his first visit to London. Accompanied by Octavius Gilchrist, he travelled by the Regent coach to 'The George and Blue Boar' at Holborn. For Clare, who had never before travelled more than twenty-five miles from his home village, the trip to London was an epic undertaking:

> my mind was full of expectations all the way about the wonders of the town which I had often heard my parents tell storys about by the winter fire and when I turnd to the recolections of the past by seeing people at my old occupations of ploughing and ditching in the fields by the road side while I was lolling in a coach the novelty created such strange feelings that I could almost fancy that my identity as well as my occupations had changed that I was

> not the same John Clare but that some stranger soul had jumpd into my skin[9]

During his time in London Clare stayed with Gilchrist's German brother-in-law, John Christian Burkhardt, who kept a jeweller's and watchmaker's shop in the Strand. He was taken to the theatre, visited Poets' Corner in Westminster Abbey, and he was entertained by John Taylor at literary dinner parties where he met a number of influential writers. He also had his portrait painted by William Hilton (at the request of John Taylor), and was introduced to Lord Radstock and Eliza Louisa Emmerson, who were to become two of his most influential patrons.

Lord Radstock – formerly Admiral the Honourable William Waldegrave – was the second son of the third Earl Waldegrave, and had received his title after an active and distinguished career in the Royal Navy. He was the author of two books: *The Cottager's Friend* and *The British Flag Triumphant*, and was known and respected in the literary and artistic circles of London. During his first visit to London, Clare was almost constantly in Lord Radstock's company. Having made enquiries about Clare, Radstock was satisfied that the poet deserved help, and took up his cause with characteristic energy.

Eliza Emmerson was the wife of a London picture importer and friend of Lord Radstock. She had a sincere admiration for Clare's work and, although her literary judgement was not always sound, she had a fairly wide knowledge of English poetry. Many kindnesses to Clare and his family were well meant, but she could at times be both interfering and almost insufferable in her behaviour. She was sentimental and theatrical, and considered herself something of a poet. She became a persistent correspondent, sending Clare well over three hundred letters.

Her attentions grew increasingly possessive and she soon told him, 'I have one wish nearer and dearer to me than another, it is to promote your fame, your welfare, your happiness! Though not the child of my adoption, you are the poet in my mind and heart.'[10]

Having spent a week in London, in a continual round of visits to dinner parties, intellectual companionship and conversation, Clare was glad to get home, back to the quiet fields and lanes of Helpston. He would visit London again, but for the time being he had had enough – he was a tired and bewildered man.

It was a few days after his return from London – on 16th March 1820 – that John Clare married Patty Turner at Great Casterton. Her uncle, John Turner, gave her away, and he and Clare's sister (Sophy) signed as witnesses; Patty's own signature was a cross, for she could neither read nor write.

Clare gives two contradictory accounts of the feelings with which he entered into matrimony. In the notes for his autobiography he implies that he did what he knew to be his duty with a heavy heart: 'I held out as long as I could and then married her at Casterton church.'[11] But in his *Sketches* he gives no hint of unwillingness: 'I had that oppertunity of easing my present trouble by making her amends I therefore made use of it and married her ... and my only repentence was that I had not become acquainted with her sooner than I did.'[12]

Patty was now six months pregnant. Yet after the wedding, bride and groom had to return separately to their parents' homes. They did not have the money to set up home together, and neither set of parents had enough room for the couple. Not until a month after the birth of their daughter (Anna Maria) on 2nd June was Clare able to 'fetch home Patty' – and then only because the occupiers of the tenement next door to his parents moved out and Parker Clare applied to the landlord for the tenancy on his son's behalf.

The circumstances attending Clare's marriage to Patty were not such as would tend to harmony. The local gossip about Patty's condition, the anger of her parents, who remained unforgiving, Clare's increasing poverty, and the necessity of starting their married life in separate establishments, were bound to create tensions for them both. Also, in spite of the fact that he had married Patty, his passionate feelings towards Mary Joyce did not weaken but, on the contrary, they grew even stronger. This was clearly a source of deep conflict and difficulty for him.

The lost Mary seems to have become his Muse, the divine transcendent source of his own creative power, who would often appear in his dreams. He records:

> these dreams of a beautiful presence a woman deity gave the sublimest conceptions of beauty to my imagination and being last night with the same presence – the lady-divinity left such a vivid picture of her visits in my sleep dreaming of dreams that I could no longer doubt her existence so I wrote them down to prolong the happiness of my faith in believing her my guardian genius[13]

He wrote many love poems to Mary, and in order to conceal her identity he used asterisks. This may have been to protect Mary herself, or it may have been purely conventional. In any case, Patty could not read, and Mary was his *Muse*, not his mistress.

The publicity given to Clare by magazines and newspapers had brought upon him a host of visitors and correspondents, some moved by a genuine desire to help and befriend, others by a passing curiosity to know more about this Northamptonshire Peasant. In the spring of 1820 he was visited by the Bishop of Peterborough, Dr Herbert Marsh, who had been persuaded by his German wife Marianne to take an interest in Clare. She had read of his success and struggles and, according to Frederick Martin, she was 'so eager in her desire to afford assistance as to induce her husband to drive over into the obscure village, and give Clare his episcopal blessing, together with half a dozen bottles of good port wine.'[14] The Bishop himself was not particularly impressed with either Helpston or the poet, but this did not prevent his wife continuing her support, nor did he object when she invited Clare to be their guest at the Bishop's Palace. She visited Helpston frequently, always taking with her parcels of food and clothing for Patty and the family.

Throughout the spring and early summer Clare received a number of visitors. He records that one day he was on his way home, looking 'shabby and dirty', when a stranger stopped him and asked if he could direct him to the poet Clare's cottage. The stranger was Chauncy Hare Townshend, who was then a student at Cambridge. To the intense surprise of his visitor, Clare declared that he himself was the poet, and offered to show him the way to his cottage. At first the stranger did not believe him, and for a few moments the two men were tense in each other's company, but as they talked, Clare seemed to think that this stranger was different:

> he was a feeling and sensible young man he talked about Poets and poetry and the fine scenery of the lakes and other matters for a good while and when he left me he put a folded paper in my hand which I found after he was gone was a sonnet and a pound bill[15]

Plate 2

ıte 1

ıte 3

Plate 4

Plate 5

Plate 6

Plate 7

ate 8

Plate 9

ate 10

Plate 11

Plate 12

Clare was evidently worried about the impression that he had made on his visitor, for during the conversation he was, he tells us, apparently seized by that 'natural depression of spirits in the presence of strangers that took from me all power of freedom or familiarity and made me dull and silent.'[16] Later he wrote to Townshend to apologise for his behaviour:

> your first visit found me in a glowering desponding condition that often gets the sway but when I have been inspired with a pint of 'John Barleycorn' & in one of my sun shining moments you would not know me I am a new man & have too many tongues tho your first visit did not find it still I can be cheery but in my sullen fits I am defiled with the old silence of rusticity that always characterized me among my neighbours before I was known to the world[17]

They exchanged several letters during the next few months, and, despite the great social differences between them, they became good friends.

Clare continued his friendship with Gilchrist and Drury, but his visits to Stamford were not quite as frequent as they had been before his visit to London. Nevertheless, he tried to see Gilchrist and Drury at least once a week. On one visit he met a Dr Bell, 'a man of odd taste but a pleasant acquaintance'.[18] Dr Bell was a lover of books, and had compiled an anthology of jests called *The Banisher of the Blue Devils*. He had been a doctor in the army and had served in the colonies. Concerned about Clare's future as a poet and his present poverty, he wrote to Earl Spencer, who agreed to give Clare £10 a year, which was paid into a trust fund.

During the remainder of 1820, letters and tributes arrived from near and far. One invitation came from General Birch Reynardson (a descendant of Jacob Reynardson, Lord Mayor of London in 1649), who lived at Holywell Hall, just beyond Pickworth. Clare knew the house well. It stood in some of the loveliest countryside on the northern boundary of Rutland and not far from where he had often walked with Patty. This is how Clare described his visit:

> it was a pleasant day for the season and I found the scenery of Holywell very beautiful ... after looking about the gardens and the library I was sent to dinner in the Servants Hall and when it was over the housekeeper invited me into her room where the governess came and chatted in a free manner and asking me to correspond with her gave me her address the housekeeper wished me to write an address to her son in imitation of Cowpers lines on his mothers picture – the governess was a pretty impertinent girl and mischeviously familiar to a mind less romantic than my own[19]

Later in the evening, when he was setting out on his homeward journey, he was even more surprised to find the young lady waiting for him outside the park. She asked if she could walk part of the way with him, and did not wait for an answer.

> I felt evil apprehensions as to her meaning but I was clownish and shoy and threatened no advantages to interpret it she chatted about my poems and resumed the discourse of wishing me to correspond with her which I promised I would when we came to the brink of the heath

> that stands in view of Patty's cottage I made a stop to get rid of her but she lingerd and chatted on till it grew very late[20]

The seduction continued until 'it grew between the late & early', and Clare hastily bid her goodnight. It was, he said, 'one of the odest adventures my poetical life met with and it made me rather conceited as I fancyd the young lady had fallen in love with me.'[21] He never mentioned her name; but we know she came from Birmingham, and must have found Clare a very attractive man!

Soon after his visit to Holywell Hall, Clare received news from London that Lord Radstock's efforts were at last bearing fruit. In January 1820 he had set up a subscription fund to provide the poet with a settled income, and by the end of April had collected nearly £200. To this was added £100 from Earl Fitzwilliam, and an advance of a further £100 from Taylor and Hessey.

By the end of the summer, Taylor had appointed Richard Woodhouse, a young lawyer, to act as a trustee. The money was then invested in the Navy Five Per Cents with the intention of providing Clare with a regular half yearly dividend, to be paid through his publishers. To begin with, this realized for him about £18 a year, which, with the annuity of £10 from Earl Spencer, and £15 from the Marquis of Exeter, gave Clare an annual income of about £43.

With what appeared to be an assured and regular income Clare might well have felt that his financial worries were over. But it was a false sense of security, because most of his 'wealth' was no more than figures on paper. It was not ready cash on which he could draw to meet the growing needs of his family. The receipts for the sale of *Poems Descriptive of Rural Life and Scenery* were never enough to combat rising prices; but the praise that Clare received during the early months of 1820 had lifted him out of his depression and despondency and, in the excitement of finding himself the author of a successful collection of poems, he began to think more positively about the future.

NOTES

1. Mark Storey (ed.): *Clare: The Critical Heritage,* pages 94-97
2. *John Clare by Himself,* page 120
3. J.W. & Anne Tibble: *John Clare: A Life* (2nd edition, Michael Joseph, 1972) page 112
4. *John Clare by Himself,* page 118
5. *Ibid.*
6. *Ibid.*
7. *Ibid.*
8. *Ibid.* page 120
9. *Ibid.* page 134
10. British Museum: *Egerton Folios* 2245-48
11. *John Clare by Himself,* page 112
12. *Ibid.* page 28
13. *Ibid.* page 254
14. Frederick W. Martin: *The Life of John Clare,* page 174
15. *John Clare by Himself,* page 128
16. *Ibid.* page 127
17. Mark Storey (ed.): *The Letters of John Clare,* page 63
18. *John Clare by Himself,* page 110
19. *Ibid.* pages 128-129
20. *Ibid.* page 130
21. *Ibid.*

CHAPTER 5

'A neglected rhymer'

The first few weeks of 1821, however, did not bring Clare the happiest start to the New Year. The success of his poetry had not resulted in the financial security he had hoped for. The money was slow in coming through; as will be explained later, it sometimes did not come through at all. His family had all shared with him some of winter's illnesses; the bad weather had kept him indoors for longer periods than he could bear, and prolonged periods of depression made the fields, which had been so reliable a source of pleasure, inaccessible even to his imagination.

Throughout the winter Clare spent much time in reading and writing. He had arranged with Taylor and Hessey to bring out another volume of poetry in the spring, but this gave rise to a number of difficulties. He wanted to call his new collection *Ways in a Village*, but had been persuaded by his publishers to call it *The Village Minstrel*. The title poem was a long one which he had started in 1819 and in which he attempted to describe his own feelings and love for village life. It contains moving descriptions of the rural poor, with poignant evocations of the old village landscape of open fields, transformed by enclosure during Clare's youth.

It was Taylor's intention to publish the work with some artistic embellishments, including a portrait of the author and a sketch of his cottage; but Clare was not entirely happy with this arrangement, possibly because the engravings were poor. On the other hand, Taylor and Hessey wished to exclude some of the poems, which they did not think quite as good as the rest, under the pretence that they had already more than sufficient in hand to make a substantial volume, but this was opposed by the author, who sent in his ultimatum to print all his verses or none.

On 2nd June 1821 Patty gave birth to their second child, but the infant (another daughter) died within a few days, leaving Clare with an ominous feeling of loss. Helpston seemed no longer to hold the same security, hope or warmth. His neighbours had grown more distant since his rise to fame, and he had become a stranger in his own village.

After some lengthy correspondence between Clare and his publishers, it was agreed that *The Village Minstrel* should be published in two volumes in the summer. This made it possible to include all the poems, with an Introduction by John Taylor, and to finish the engravings with the care desired by the author. Meanwhile, to keep Clare before the public, extracts of the forthcoming work were published at intervals in the *London Magazine*, and finally, the September edition contained the announcement that '*The Village Minstrel* and other poems by John Clare, the Northamptonshire Peasant, with a fine portrait, will be published in a few days.'[1] It was eventually published towards the end of September 1821.

Throughout the autumn, Clare continued to receive visitors. In a letter to John Taylor he said that had he known four years ago that he would ever have so much flattery he would surely have died of vanity: '… let me wait another year or two & t[he] peep show will be over – & my vani[ty] if I have any will end in its proper mortification to know that obscurity is happiness & that John Clare the thresher in the onset & neglected ryhmer in the end are the only two comfortable periods of his life.'[2]

There was no reason at that time to suppose that Clare would become a 'neglected rhymer', yet within a few months he was to see his prophecy beginning to come true, for by December only eight hundred copies of *The Village Minstrel* had been sold, and it was evident that it would not achieve a sale comparable with that of his first volume. This was felt as little short of disastrous by Clare; he was afraid his fame was proving short-lived, and his bouts of depression increased in severity.

By the time the third and fourth editions of *Poems Descriptive of Rural Life and Scenery* appeared there had been several changes in the contents. The original edition had contained 'vulgarities', 'indelicacies', accusations against the rich and sentiments of 'ingratitude' which offended the minds of people like Lord Radstock and Eliza Emmerson. As early as 12th February 1820 Taylor had written to Clare to say that Lord Radstock and others were objecting to poems such as 'The Country Girl', 'My Mary', 'Dolly's Mistake', 'Friend Lubin', 'Dawnings of Genius' and 'Helpstone'. Not only were they objecting, they were also insisting that these poems should be omitted from all future editions.

On 11th May Lord Radstock wrote to Eliza Emmerson: '*You must do your duty!* You must tell [Clare] – to expunge certain highly objectionable passages in the first volume ... passages, wherein, his then depressed state hurried him not only into error, but into the most flagrant acts of injustice; by accusing those of pride, cruelty, vices, and ill-directed passions – who are the very persons, by whose truly generous and noble exertions he has been raised from misery ... tell Clare if he has still a recollection of what I have done, and am still doing for him, he must give me unquestionable proofs of being that man I would have him be – he must expunge!'[3]

Eliza Emmerson immediately took up the matter and wrote to Clare: 'Let me entreat you, as a true friend – as a sister – to write immediately to Mr Taylor and desire him *from yourself* to expunge the objectionable lines – you have them marked in the volume I sent you – for alas! they were named to me too soon after your poems were published – as conveying Radical and Ungrateful sentiments.'[4]

The following lines were deleted from 'Helpstone' because Lord Radstock objected to their 'radical slang':

> Oh! who could see my dear green willows fall,
> What feeling heart, but dropt a tear for all?
> Accursed Wealth! o'er-bounding human laws,
> Of every evil thou remain'st the cause:
> Victims of want, those wretches such as me,
> Too truly lay their wretchedness to thee:
> Thou art the bar that keeps from being fed,
> And thine our loss of labour and of bread;
> Thou art the cause that levels every tree,
> And woods bow down to clear a way for thee.

'Radical' opinions were considered dangerous because of the fear of political agitation and violence they might unleash. Popular radicalism was motivated by a deep-rooted 'common-sense' of the rights of labour: to affordable food, to customary rights, and a determination to protect and, if need be, to fight for these things. Although Clare never associated himself with violent reform, he used the language of protest to express his outrage at the way in which the rural poor had been victimized by the ruling class.

Radstock's demand that 'radical' and 'indelicate' lines should be expunged was a clear indication of social and political pressures censoring freedom of expression in literature. He judged the offending lines with an eye more upon their moral and political allegiance than upon their literary merit.

Clare did not set out to shock or offend, only to be honest. He was using words which were in common usage among the people with whom he worked; they were part of their natural vocabulary. In rural areas, words considered 'indelicate' or 'bad language' (such as 'arse', which, to Clare's ear, was more tuneful than its alternatives) were more often used as words of endearment, or were of such ancient tradition as to be acceptable.

Clare pleaded his case to Taylor when he wrote: 'The language of nature ... can never be disgusting ... I heartily desire no word of mine to be altered.'[5] He had argued that a poet's vocabulary is important to him. It is only when he finds his 'own voice' that his work becomes original and alive. He did not want to imitate, or dilute the richness of his vocabulary to please others. Taylor tried to understand this, and Clare, in return, tried to trust his judgement, but both men were under enormous pressure.

Eliza Emmerson, who could not appreciate Clare's arguments, wanted to rewrite some of his lines for him. She requested alterations on many occasions, and was always urging him away from his natural style to 'loftier regions of poetry'. She wrote to him: 'Your subject will afford you good scope for simple and sweet description, also matter and opportunity for much reflection – 'tis in *these* you *excel* ...'[6] Later she sent a flattering note in which she said, 'Your 'Peasant Boy' is uniformly sweet and simple ...

your sonnets – ah! there my dear friend – you stand alone, you are yourself – all simplicity – all feeling and soul.'[7]

Clare was always being reminded of his position, still being kept in his place. His sensitive nature was aware of these attitudes, even if he could not always see that he was being manipulated by his patrons. He was grateful for their good intentions; but he was not so pleased always to be the 'Peasant Poet'. All he was ever to get for his 'simple verses' was a charitable handout. Most of the money he received was because he was an unusual *peasant* rather than an extraordinary poet. But he did not want charity; all he wanted was true recognition. The occasional payments made by his publishers seemed to him no better than being kept by the parish.

On his walks and at his work Clare enjoyed solitude, but at other times he felt an acute loneliness, for, although he seems to have been happy at home, there was no one there with whom he could discuss his poetry or the books he read. Patty, unable to read or write, knew no more of poetry than the average farmer's daughter, and his parents were always preoccupied with their declining health.

Clare had, however, two good friends on whom he relied greatly at this time, wandering the fields or talking over their common interests; both men were servants at Milton Hall. There was Edmund Tyrell Artis, the butler, who was an archaeologist in his spare time, and was always busy with Roman coins or bits of pottery that he had unearthed, while Joseph Henderson, the head gardener, was a keen botanist. Clare had met both men in 1820 on his first visit to Milton Hall and had found them to be sympathetic, interesting companions. Both men were well read and could talk about poetry for hours. He wrote of these friends:

> I never met with a party of more happy and hearti[e]r fellows in my life ... There was Artis up to the neck in the old Norman Coins and broken pots of the Romans and Henderson never wearied with hunting after the Emperor Butterfly and the Hornet Sphinx in the Hanglands wood and the Orchises on the Heath[8]

Clare spent three days at Milton in January 1822 studying Roman remains with Artis, which gave him some respite from his work. On returning to Helpston he began to explore the possibility of acquiring 'Bachelors Hall', which included a piece of freehold land of about seven acres, close to his cottage. The Billings brothers, who owned it, were unable to keep up the repayments on a £200 mortgage, and were in danger of being evicted from their old home. They were Clare's friends, and he wanted to help them by taking over the mortgage and saving 'Bachelors Hall' for them – and for himself.

To get the £200 required he approached Lord Radstock, whom he looked upon as one of his warmest and most sincere friends. He did not want to borrow the money, but to take it from the sum standing in his name in the funds set up by his patrons. But Radstock told him this could not be done, as the sum of £240 was invested in the name of trustees who had no power to withdraw any portion of this amount.

Although he was disappointed, Clare did not give up the struggle for his great object. His next attempt was to get the required £200 from his publisher, John Taylor, to whom he offered, in return, to sell the copyright of all his poems for the next five years. And so on 31st January 1822 he wrote to Taylor:

> the Cottage is a beautiful spot of 6 or 7 Acres there are crowds for it if it be sold but if I could get hold of the mortgage it would be mine & still doing a kindness to a friend I should like to make sure of it as 'Poets Hall' instead of 'Bachelors' which must soon be extinct if I dont succeed – Ill do this way if you like Ill sell you my writings for five years for that sum which cant be dear[9]

Taylor, however, felt that this was a preposterous scheme, and finally it was left to Lord Milton to pay off the arrears of £20 interest and keep the Billings brothers as tenants for a few more years.

Having failed to become a property owner, Clare was despondent and began to overwork himself. This mood persisted throughout February and March. On 16th March he wrote to James Hessey about the 'confounded lethargy of low spirits that presses on me to such a degree that at times makes me feel as if my senses had a mind to leave me Spring & Fall such feelings it seems are doomd to be my companions but it shall not overpowr me as formerly with such weak & terrible dreads & fears of dropping off when death comes he will come & while lifes mine Ill make the best of it.'[10]

Clare realised that he needed to get away from Helpston, if only for a few weeks. Eliza Emmerson certainly thought, from the correspondence she had had with him during the winter, that he needed a holiday and invited him to stay with her at her new home in London. He was only too eager to accept. James Hessey also shared her feelings and wrote to Clare suggesting that he should spend the first few days in Fleet Street with his publishers before going to the Emmersons.

And so in early summer of 1822 Clare set out on his second

visit to London. He had hoped that Octavius Gilchrist would again be able to travel with him, but he was too ill to leave home and told Clare he must travel alone. It was not the most comfortable of journeys. The weather was bad and the roads in poor condition: 'We went 20 miles & upwards in the most dreadfull thunderstorm I ever witnessed & the rain was very heavy & lashing ...'[11] But he arrived safely and was soon caught up again in the excitement of the Capital. He could enjoy himself without family responsibilities inhibiting his sense of freedom.

Clare stayed in London for three weeks. His daily routine was to spend the morning reading all the new books within his reach, and during the afternoon and evening he had exhilarating conversations with some of the literary figures of the day, and, from his observations, left some vivid impressions of the men he dined with:

> Hazlitt ... sits a silent picture of severity if you was to watch his face for a month you would not catch a smile there ... when he enters a room he comes stooping with his eyes in his hands as it were throwing under gazes round at every corner as if he smelt a dun or thief ready to seize him by the collar and demand his money or his life he is [a] middle sizd dark looking man and his face is deeply lind with a satirical character his eyes are bright but they are rather turned under his brows he is a walking satire and you would wonder where his poetry came from that is scatterd so thickly over his writings for the blood of me I coud not find him out that is I should have had no guess at him of his ever being a scribbler much more a genius ...
>
> ... then there is Charles Lamb a long remove from his friend Hazlitt in ways and manners he is very fond of

> snuff which seems to sharpen up his wit every time he dips his plentiful finger into his large bronse colourd box and then he sharpens up his head thro[w]s himself backward in his chair and stammers at a joke or pun with an inward sort of utterance ere he can give it speech … at last he leans off with scarcly 'good night' in his mouth and disapears leaving his memory like a pleasant ghost hanging about his vacant chair …
>
> … and there sits Cary the translator of Dante one of the most quiet amiable and unasuming of men he will look round the table in a peaceful silence on all the merry faces in all the vacant unconser[n]ment imaginable and then he will brighten up and look smilingly on you …[12]

There were others, too, such as Thomas de Quincey, 'the Opium Eater and that abstruse thinker in Logic', who was 'a little artless simple seeming body somthing of a child over grown in a blue coat and black neckerchief for his dress is singular with his hat in his hands steals gently among the company with a smile timidly round the room.'[13] And there was J.H. Reynolds, who was always the life and soul of the party: 'he was the most good natured fellow I ever met with his face was the three in one of fun wit and punning personified … he would punch you with his puns very keenly without ever hurting your feelings … nothing could put him out of humour either with himself or others … his teeth are always looking through a laugh that sits as easy on his unpuckerd lips as if he was born laughing.'[14]

All the problems back home seemed as far away as a forgotten dream; this was a new life, and Clare wanted to enjoy every moment of it. Sadly, it did not last. After three weeks, he arrived home to find that Patty had given birth to another daughter on

13th June. She was named Eliza Louisa, after her godmother Eliza Emmerson, who sent a silver cup and other gifts and later paid for the child's education. Patty was so ill as to cause considerable anxiety for a few days.

Towards the end of 1823 Clare was again showing signs of severe depression. On 5th January 1824 his fourth child (Frederick) was born. His health improved for a while, until he realised that he had one more mouth to feed, and one more body to find room for in the cottage. His depression returned, and he was invited by John Taylor to stay with him again in London where he could receive expert medical advice.

Taylor arranged for him to see Dr George Darling, the eminent Scottish physician. Clare recorded that he was suffering from phobias – he was seeing 'thin, death-like shadows and goblins with saucer eyes'. Passers-by were supernatural agents 'whose errands might be to carry me away at the first dark alley we came to.'[15] He expected to meet Death or the Devil in Chancery Lane. Developing morbid fears of future decay and death, he began to lose control of his mental processes.

Under Dr Darling's treatment Clare's bodily health improved, but mentally he was far from well. The physician insisted that his patient should have a complete rest, that he should not get over-excited or involved in too much deep conversation, and that his drinking habits should stop. He attributed much of Clare's illness to his own anxiety; he was far too ambitious and wanted immediate success. Naturally he wanted his work to be accepted and praised, and his recognition as a poet to be confirmed. But, coming from his humble background, it was intellectually and emotionally exhausting for the Northamptonshire Peasant to compete in this way. Even the dinner parties demanded more of Clare than they did of everyone else. People such as John Taylor, William Hazlitt and Charles Lamb were eloquent men who could relax in their after-dinner discussions, but not Clare. He enjoyed their company and could participate a little in their conversation, but he was always tense, always watchful, believing that he was on trial, and by the end of the evening he was exhausted.

It was clear to Dr Darling that Clare's feelings of inferiority, insecurity and despair were making him ill. He therefore advised him to give up all expectations of acquiring fame or wealth as a poet, saying that it would be wise for him to return to his old occupation as a labourer and write verses only during his leisure hours. This seemed extremely hard to Clare, but he was faced with Dr Darling's opinion that there was no longer any real demand for poetry among the people at large.

After nearly two months in London, Clare was well enough to attend Taylor's literary dinner parties, at which he met many eminent authors of the day. On 14th July Clare happened to be walking along Oxford Street on his way to see Eliza Emmerson, when he observed a small crowd that had gathered to see Lord Byron's funeral cortège as it crossed London on its way to Newstead Abbey in Nottinghamshire. As the procession came into sight, a young girl who was standing beside Clare gave a deep sigh and said, 'Poor Lord Byron!' This is how Clare records the occasion:

> I lookd up in the young girls face it was dark and beautiful and I could almost feel in love with her for the sigh she had utterd for the poet it was worth all the News paper puffs and Magazine Mournings that ever was paraded after the death of a poet … the common people … are the veins and arterys that feed and quicken the heart of living fame

> ... the streets were lind as the procession passd on each side but they were all the commonest and lowest orders[16]

For Clare, Byron, whose greatness was beyond doubt, shared the feelings of the common people who recognised his merits, and who 'felt by a natural impulse that the mighty was fallen and they mourned in saddened silence.'[17] This event left a deep impression on Clare's mind.

Dr Darling now believed that the place for Clare was back home among the trees and meadows of his native landscape, where he might still find some peace and security. And so he left London on 8th August, after promising that he would give up drinking entirely. That promise was faithfully kept for several years to come. He never visited a public house, and even at home he drank little else but water and weak tea and coffee.

Clare had been away from Helpston for about ten weeks, and it was with a lifting heart that he saw again the familiar church spire above the trees, and the fields coloured with ripening corn, all ready for harvest. Whatever he thought about London, it was here that he belonged, here he was happiest. As he approached Helpston in the evening, far removed from the noise and bustle of Fleet Street, his keen eye and ear must have been delighted.

But there were new struggles ahead. Back once more in Helpston, he had to face the responsibilities of providing food for his growing family. His reputation as a poet met with increasing indifference among his neighbours. He earnestly sought work and, though sneered at by one or two farmers who told him that he was 'too famous' to soil his hands, he at last secured employment on Helpston Heath, part of which was being enclosed for the benefit of the rich landowners. Clare despised enclosure but, as he was in desperate need, it was this or nothing.

Since there was not enough work for all the villagers, 'catch-work gangs' were congregated and tramped off to any farmer who required them. They often had to sleep out in the open fields; this was not ideal employment for a married man with a family, and it was certainly not good for Clare's health. So after just a few days he returned home, and the search for work once again became a priority.

NOTES

1. Mark Storey (ed.): *Clare: The Critical Heritage*, page 136
2. Mark Storey (ed.): *The Letters of John Clare*, page 215
3. British Museum, *Egerton Folios*, 2245-48
4. *Ibid.*
5. Peterborough Manuscripts (Peterborough Museum)
6. British Museum, *Egerton Folios*, 2245-48
7. *Ibid.*
8. *John Clare by Himself*, page 130
9. Mark Storey (ed.): *The Letters of John Clare*, pages 227-228
10. *Ibid.* page 234
11. *John Clare by Himself*, page 146
12. *Ibid.* page 142-144
13. *Ibid.* page 144
14. *Ibid.* page 140
15. *Ibid.* page 155
16. *Ibid.* pages 156-157
17. *Ibid.* page 157

CHAPTER 6

'Let truth attend the rhyme'

Between 1809 and 1824, with the passage of the act of parliament enclosing the open commons of Helpston and several neighbouring parishes, Clare had seen a radical transformation of the old open field landscape around Helpston. In the creation of a new topography, trees were cut down, ancient common rights of grazing and collecting firewood were annulled, new roads and systems of drainage were constructed, and the land was divided into square parcels marked off by new hedges and fences.

Enclosure meant that the whole of Clare's native landscape was to disappear under the plough. 'A landscape whose "only bondage was the circling sky" was being fenced and staked out for somebody else's gain.'[1] He witnessed the increasing economic distress of the agricultural labourer, his frequent dependence upon parish relief to maintain even a bare subsistence level, and the seemingly parallel increase in prosperity of the independent farmer and landowner. Clare hated and despised enclosure, not just for its economic effects, but also for the changes it brought to the social life of the village:

how many days have passd since we usd to hunt the stag
or hunt the slipper but there usd to be one crook horn

> [= game] etc in those days and duck under water on May eve and tossing the cowslip balls over the garland that hung from chimney to chimney across the street and then there was going to east well on a sunday to drink sugar and water at the spring head but enclosure came and drove these from the village[2]

The two conditions – despoliation of a native environment, and economic deprivation – fused into a single perception: a sense that traditional values had fragmented, that the very identity of an old rural experience was being fast destroyed. In 'Remembrances' he shows how memory was desecrated by the act of enclosure:

> By Langley bush I roam but the bush hath left its hill
> On cowper green I stray tis a desert strange and chill
> And spreading lea close oak ere decay had penned its
> will
> To the axe of the spoiler and self-interest fell a prey
> And cross berry way and old round oaks narrow lane
> With its hollow trees like pulpits I shall never see again
> Inclosure like a Buonaparte let not a thing remain
> It levelled every bush and tree and levelled every hill
> And hung the moles for traitors – though the brook is
> running still
> It runs a naked brook cold and chill[3]

'The effect,' writes John Barrell, 'is to make the enclosure seem to have been as inevitable as is the loss of childhood and the pleasures of childhood; and the bare landscape of Helpston after the enclosure becomes also a land now stripped by time of its pleasant associations, and now no more than a collection of impersonal things.'[4]

For the poor, the central issue of enclosure was not agricultural efficiency but trespass; local landowners forcibly barred people from crossing their land. It usually meant heavy losses for the people, both of common land and footpaths:

> There once were lanes in nature's freedom dropt,
> There once were paths that every valley wound –
> Inclosure came, and every path was stopt;
> Each tyrant fix'd his sign where paths were found,
> To hint a tresspass now who cross'd the ground:
> Justice is made to speak as they command;
> The high road now must be each stinted bound;
> – Inclosure, thou'rt a curse upon the land,
> And tasteless was the wretch who thy existence plann'd[5]

Such changes would have been profoundly disturbing to the natives of the place, most of all to one whose poetic inspiration sprang from it. In his *Journal* for September 1824 Clare records that he 'took a walk in the fields ... saw an old woodstile taken away from a favourite spot which it had occupied all my life ... the posts were over grown with ivy and it seemed so akin to nature and the spot where it stood as tho it had taken it on lease for an undisturbed existence ... it hurt me to see it was gone ... for my affections claims a friendship with such things.'[6]

When he writes of enclosure Clare recognises the affront to nature involved in a further intrusion of the man-made into nature's domain. His lament for the old village structures of Helpston is on behalf of the poor labourers depossessed of their rights; but it is also on behalf of the cattle who will no longer be able to wander freely over the common land. In condemning the enclosure he also looks back and preserves in his poetry the landscape that had been lost:

Far spread the moorey ground a level scene
Bespread with rush and one eternal green
That never felt the rage of blundering plough
Though centurys wreathed spring's blossoms on its brow
Still meeting plains that stretched them from far away
In uncheckt shadows of green, brown and grey
Unbounded freedom ruled the wandering scene
Nor fence of ownership crept in between
To hide the prospect of the following eye
Its only bondage was the circling sky
One mighty flat undwarfed by bush and tree
Spread its faint shadow of immensity
And lost itself which seemed to eke its bounds
In the blue mist the orisons edge surrounds
Now this sweet vision of my boyish hours
Free as spring clouds and wild as summer flowers
Is faded all – a hope that blossomed free
And hath been once, no more shall ever be
Inclosure came and trampled on the grave
Of labours rights and left the poor a slave[7]

To Clare, enclosure was a sign of the whole moral perversity of the enclosing class. It not only destroyed the labourer's access to the land but made him act as the agent of the very process that had victimized him, since it was the *labourer* and not the property owner who had to do the actual work of draining, levelling and fencing the old landscape.

Clare's bitterness was personal. He wrote with anger and contempt. By early 1823 he had written *The Parish*, a long satirical poem of over two thousand lines, and in a manuscript note he gives a revealing account of the emotional condition in which the work was drafted:

> This poem was begun & finished under the pressure of heavy distress with embittred feelings under a state of anxiety & oppression almost amounting to slavery – when the prosperity of one class was founded on the adversity & distress of the other – The haughty demand by the master to his labourer was work for the little I chuse to allow you & go to the parish for the rest – or starve – to decline working under such advantages was next to offending a magistrate & no oppertunity was lost in marking the insult by some unqualified oppression[8]

Clare worked on *The Parish* over a period of many years, and in 1826 he thought it was 'the best thing in my own mind that I have ever written'.[9] The poem is taken up with the evil social effects of enclosure, the inflationary agriculture of the Napoleonic Wars, and the changed status of the local Anglican parson. *The Parish* is the fullest available picture of the new order which had succeeded the old. As many of the characters demonstrate, there had arisen 'a pigmy reigning race', notable only for the hypocrisy and tyranny of its attitudes, the squalid immorality of its way of life. It is a vitriolic and energetic satire on the corruption and pretentions of developments in village life, revealing the intensity of Clare's political and moral critique of rural culture in the wake of the enclosure movement. *The Parish* begins:

The Parish hind oppressions humble slave
Whose only hopes of freedom is the grave
The cant miscalled religion in the saint
And Justice mockd while listning wants complaint
The parish laws and parish queens and kings
Prides lowest classes of pretending things
The meanest dregs of tyranny and crime
I fearless sing let truth attend the ryhme[10]

The names of the characters tell their own story: they are 'farmers of the New & Old School a village politician & Steward ... a Justice of the peace &c &c ...'[11] There is Miss Peevish Scornful, the farmer's daughter, given to fashion and tittle-tattle, Squire Dandy, 'just returned from France' ready to woo every girl in the parish, Farmer Bigg, young Headlong Racket, Dandy Flint Esquire, proud Farmer Cheetum, Old Saveall, Young Bragg; they are the principal members of a corrupt society, which includes a whole pyramid of tyrants:

Churchwardens Constables and Overseers
Makes up the round of Commons and of Peers
With learning just enough to sign a name
And skill sufficient parish rates to frame
And cunning deep enough the poor to cheat[12]

The Parish is at its best when satirizing religion. Clare was brought up in the Church of England, but in his youth he joined the Independents (Congregational dissenters) in his search for a more acceptable form of religion than that of the Established Church, which never found much time for the poor. In the 1820s he attended both Wesleyan and Primitive Methodist meetings, and after reading the works of Richard Wright the Unitarian missionary, he talked of becoming a Unitarian. He was also interested in the Quakers. Clare was tolerant of other people's beliefs, provided they in turn were not intolerant. He wanted to see all Christians united in a common faith which expressed itself in love and service to those in need, whatever their race or creed.

In 1824 Clare was in a state of religious turmoil. He was looking for a religious community to which he might belong with more enthusiasm than he was able to find in the Anglican Church. Its soothing ritual of fine prayers satisfied his feelings for tradition and poetry, but he considered its members to be 'prone to cant and humbug'. He was quick to condemn hypocrisy and insincerity in religion, and in a letter to John Taylor expressed his feelings:

> the religious hypocrite is the worst monster in human nature & some of these when they had grown so flagrant as to be discovered behind the mask they had taken to shelter their wickedness led me first to think lightly of religion & sure enough some of the lower classes of dissenters about us are very decietful & in fact dangerous characters especially among the methodists with whom I have determind not to associate but then there are a many sincere good ones to make up ... my opinion ... of true Religion amounts to this ... if a man turns to god with real sincerity of heart and not canting & creeping to the eyes of the world but satisfying his own conscidence so that it shall not upbraid him in the last hours of life that touchstone of faith & practice careless of what the world may say either for him or against him that man in my opinion is as certain of heaven in the next world as he is of death in this[13]

Later he wrote: 'A religion that teaches us to act justly and to speak truth and love mercy ought to be held sacred in every country and what ever the differences of creeds may be in higher matters they ought to be overlooked and the principle respected.'[14] He had 'turned methodist', but he found 'the lower orders of this persuasion ... so selfish and narrow minded and ignor[ant] of real religion that [he] soon left them.'[15] Frustrated with the Established Church, he contemplated joining the Ranters (Primitive Methodists who had broken away from the Wesleyan Methodists). Taylor advised Clare to 'get real practical Religion wherever it can be found.'[16]

A little later, on 20th April 1824, Clare wrote to James Hessey: 'I have joined the Ranters ... that is I have enlisted in their society ... they are a set of simple sincere & communing christians with more zeal than knowledge earnest & happy in their devotions ... O that I could feel as they do but I cannot ... their affection for each other ... their earnest tho simple extempore prayers puts my dark unsettled conscience to shame.'[17] He provides Hessey with a detailed account of how the Ranters spend their sabbath, and then adds: '... my feelings are so unstrung in their company that I can scarcely refrain from shedding tears & when I went [to] church I coud scarcely refrain from sleep.'[18]

Religion had fallen on evil days. It had become 'little more than cant/A cloak to hide what godliness may want':

[Men] love mild sermons with few threats perplexd
And then deem it sinful to forget the text
They turn to business ere they leave the church
And linger oft to comment in the porch
Of fresh rates wanted from the needy poor
And list of taxes naild upon the door

Little religion in each bosom dwells ...
The drunken cobler leaves his wicked life
Hastes to save others and neglects his wife[19]

The new vicar encouraged class distinction by visiting only the rich and riding most weekdays with the hounds, instead of caring for the pastoral needs of his parish. Old Ralph, 'the veriest rake the town possessed' – converted, turned preacher – was well on the way to sainthood; but 'a simpering Eve crept into his garden'; he fell, and after leading a double life for some time, was found out by his flock, and the new-born saint became the old sinner again.

Behind the clamour for reform raised by 'squire-aping farmers', Clare saw lurking the wolf of self interest. Power might change hands, but the poor would not benefit; as in France, the cause of freedom would become a tyrant's tool. The village politician, as Clare saw him, was often a tyrant on a small scale:

Who votes equality that all men share
And stints the pauper of his parish fare
Who damns all taxes both of church & state
And on the parish lays a double rate[20]

Clare bore witness to the overthrow of the social order of the past. There arose a new breed of prosperous farmer who scorned tradition and no longer sat down with his men at the supper table at harvest time. Trees were cut down, coppices destroyed, and streams were diverted from their natural courses – all in the name of 'progress' and 'improvement'. The wild life that Clare had reverenced for so long was victim too. The 'birds and beasts of fate's despised birth' were

Forced from the wilds which nature left their home
By vile invasions of encroaching men[21]

NOTES

1. Edward Storey: *A Right to Song*, page 94
2. *John Clare by Himself*, page 46
3. *The Oxford Authors: John Clare*, edited by Eric Robinson & David Powell, page 260
4. John Barrell: *The Idea of Landscape and the Sense of Place 1730-1840: An Approach to the Poetry of John Clare*, page 175
5. From 'The Village Minstrel' in J.W. & Anne Tibble: *John Clare: Selected Poems*, page 50
6. *John Clare by Himself*, page 79
7. From 'The Mores' – *The Oxford Authors: John Clare*, page 167
8. *The Parish*, edited by Eric Robinson, page 27
9. J.W. & Anne Tibble: *The Letters of John Clare*, page 192
10. *The Parish*, page 31
11. Tibble: *The Letters of John Clare*, page 140
12. *The Parish*, page 62
13. Mark Storey (ed.): *The Letters of John Clare*, page 292
14. *John Clare by Himself*, page 134
15. *Ibid*. page 133
16. Mark Storey (ed.): *The Letters of John Clare*, page 291
17. *Ibid*. page 294
18. *Ibid*.
19. *The Parish*, page 43
20. *Ibid*. page 57
21. *Ibid*.

CHAPTER 7

Hopes and Fears

In the autumn of 1825, Clare's main preoccupation was with *The Shepherd's Calendar,* which he had been discussing with his publisher for many years. In January 1820, less than a week after the appearance of *Poems Descriptive of Rural Life and Scenery,* John Taylor had written to him greatly approving his idea for a poem to be entitled 'A Week in a Village'. In order to create an overall structure for the work, Taylor had suggested he might

> divide the Week's Employment into the 7 days, selecting such for each as might particularly apply to that Day, which is the Case with some of the Occupations:– that the remaining which might be pursued in any Day should be allotted so as to fill up the Time; – that the Sports & Amusements should in like manner be apportioned out into the 7 days; – and that one little appropriate Story should be involved in each Day's Description.[1]

Although this particular plan was never realised, Taylor's proposal for a poem of considerable length was not forgotten, and over three years later he wrote to Clare with a variation upon his earlier suggestion:

> Talking the other day with Hessey, it occurred to me that a good Title for another Work would be 'The Shepherd's Calendar' – a Name which Spenser took for a Poem or rather Collection of Poems of his. – It might be like his divided into Months, & under each might be given a descriptive Poem & a Narrative Poem.[2]

The twelve narrative pieces proposed as an accompaniment to the descriptive verse were in fact never completed; and, when the volume was eventually published, only four tales, grouped separately under the general heading of 'Village Stories', appeared.

Clare expected *The Shepherd's Calendar* to be published in the summer of 1826, but he was disappointed in his expectations. There were enough poems to make at least two volumes; but Taylor was not over anxious to publish them. A shrewd man of business, he was fully aware that the tide was turning against poetry. He had great respect for Clare, and held his talent in fair estimation from the fact that *Poems Descriptive of Rural Life and Scenery* had gone through four editions. But against this fact he was also aware that *The Village Minstrel* had not sold well. Taylor therefore resolved to treat his 'Northamptonshire Peasant' with great caution.

Clare was extremely anxious when he was told that his new volume was not to be published in the summer, nor during the remaining part of the year. He regarded this delay as a scorn on his fame, and he also felt it as the ruin of his financial prospects. So, in order to add a little to his income, he began to write for the poetry Annuals. The *Literary Souvenir* of 1826, edited by Alaric Watts, published two poems. He was also represented in the 1827 and 1828 volumes. A number of his poems, some of considerable length, appeared in *Friendship's Offering*, edited by Thomas Pringle. Then poems appeared in the *Amulet*, edited by S.C. Hall; others were printed in Ackerman's *Forget Me Not* and Thomas Hood's *Gem*. A few poems were published in newspapers and magazines of this period, but it was not much help to Clare financially, for many of the editors were unreliable in their payments, either delaying for a year before making them, or else not making them at all; and they were all apt to alter the contributions drastically and without reference to the author. In December 1825, Clare was forced to write to James Hessey: '... as to the Poetical Almanaks they may all go to Hell next year for I can get nothing by them & my contributions are so mutilated that I do not know them again.'[3]

Increasing poverty and debt were seriously affecting Clare's health, but despite such hardships his family continued to grow. On 18th June 1826, Patty gave birth to a fifth child who was baptized 'John, son of John Clare, Poet'. Within a year she gave birth again, to a child who died before it was baptized. Their second daughter, Eliza, had (like Anna Maria) started school, and Eliza Emmerson gave Patty enough money to buy them new clothes.

Clare seems to have spent the rest of the year urging Taylor to publish *The Shepherd's Calendar* without delay, but he received cold answers in return. Taylor told Clare that it was the wrong time to publish poetry, as there was a general slump in sales, and the public were not interested. Taylor had become frustrated over the whole idea. He was tired, too, of editing and copying Clare's often erratic manuscripts, and engaged Harry Van Dyk, a young poet he had recently discovered, to help with the task of preparing fair copies of the poems. Taylor felt it was necessary to edit the manuscripts, so that by the time *The*

Shepherd's Calendar eventually appeared, it had been reduced from 3,382 lines to 1,761, and Clare still had to write an alternative section on 'July' – which was nowhere as good as the original rejected by Taylor.

The Shepherd's Calendar was published in April 1827, but it sold poorly. There were a few favourable reviews. *The Literary Gazette* said it had 'a great deal of sweet poetry'[4] and *The Eclectic Review* recognised that 'the present volume, as compared with Clare's first efforts, exhibits very unequivocal signs of intellectual growth, an improved taste, and an enriched mind.'[5] But the *London Weekly Review* took a very different view:

> We happened to open this little book in so pleasant a mood, that we almost felt our judgement might be somewhat improperly biased in the estimate of its intrinsic merits. We had not, however, perused many pages before we discovered that our self-suspicions were wholly groundless. Wretched taste, poverty of thought, and uninteligible phraseology, for some time appeared its only characteristics. There was nothing, perhaps, which more provoked our spleen than the want of a glossary; for without such an assistance, how could we perceive the fitness and beauty of such words as – *crizzling* – *sliveth* – *whineys* – *greening* – *croodling* – *hings* – *progged* – *sprindling* – *siling* – *struttles* – &c ...[6]

Sales of *The Shepherd's Calendar* were worse than Taylor feared; only 425 copies were sold in the first two years. The idea of *The Shepherd's Calendar* was not original; other poets had written about the seasons, the months of the year, the yearly

Plate 13. Footpath near Etton

Plate 14. The path to Eastwell Spring

Plate 15. An old willow near Helpston

Plate 16. A 'pulpit' tree

patterns of the village and country people, and the title did not appeal to the reading public. Perhaps this was the editor's fault. Its publication did little to change Clare's fortune. He was now in desperate need of money, wishing to clear himself of debt. He was, therefore, obliged to turn to farming to support his wife, six children and aging parents. But his health was rapidly deteriorating and, in February 1828, Eliza Emmerson wrote begging him to stay with her in London. He could then discuss his literary affairs with John Taylor, and relax for a few weeks. Patty and his family were equally anxious for him to go if another stay in London would improve his health and mind.

Clare needed little persuasion, and on 24th February he set out on his fourth visit to London. What we know of it is gleaned from his letters. On 25th February he wrote to Patty:

> Mrs Emmersons Docter a Mr Ward told me last night that there was little or nothing the matter with me & yet I got no sleep the whole of last night but I hope for better success tonight ... I have as yet no medicine & perhaps I shall not but I shall most likely see Dr Darling before long for satisfaction ...[7]

Clare seems to have spent much of his time with the Emmersons at Stratford Place. He was afraid to venture far without a guide, but a guide was not always available. If he went out by himself he would turn his step towards Fleet Street and St Paul's, for that was the only part of London he knew.

One of his first visits in London was to Allan Cunningham, who was a fellow self-taught poet. Cunningham heard for the first time that Clare was in great distress, and that his poetry, far from bringing him financial security, had actually left him in debt. Filled with compassion, Cunningham offered him assistance – but this was proudly refused. He then advised Clare to see John Taylor and request, politely but firmly, an account of the profits made by the sale of his books.

Clare spoke to Taylor, but he was now busy publishing textbooks for the University of London, and wanted nothing more to do with poetry. He therefore suggested that Clare should buy up the stock of his books at greatly reduced prices and hawk them around the villages at home. Against the advice of his friends, Clare accepted the offer and thought it would be a way of making some money out of his poetic ruins. But his friends were outraged at Taylor's suggestion, and thought that no author should be subjected to such an indignity.

During this visit to London, Clare spent some time in the company of Henry Behnes, who was setting out with great determination to make his name as a sculptor. For some years to come, he worked enthusiastically on Clare's behalf, taking his poems round and extracting money from editors for them. Another result of their friendship was the bronze bust of Clare (see illustration), for which he sat during his visit.

By the middle of March, Clare was homesick, and on the 21st he wrote to Patty to announce that he would return home the following week. His subsequent departure was unexpected and sudden; he was so eager to get away from London that he left behind his overcoat and a number of books, which Eliza Emmerson had to forward by coach to the Bull Inn at Market Deeping.

Soon after his return to Helpston, Patty gave birth to a third son, who was baptized William Parker, on 4th May. The Clares now had five surviving children to keep and the poet's aging parents to support. Money was needed more than ever before. Time which could have been spent working on the land was used in vain attempts to sell his books. Even though he hawked his wares through the village streets where he was known, there were few people in and around Helpston who now wanted to buy them, and days went by without a sale being made.

Clare found it hard to accept that his popularity was over, despite the fact that he had forecast this happening. The production of *The Shepherd's Calendar* had drained much of his spirit; nightmares and illness followed. There were days when he refused to go out of the house or even rise from his bed. In the autumn, when he had almost given up hope, he was invited to Boston by Henry Brook (editor of *The Boston Gazette*) to be the guest speaker at the Mayor's annual dinner. Although Clare did not have much time for civic ceremonies, he agreed to go, and walked the thirty-six miles, carrying a supply of his books which he hoped he would be able to sell.

The people of that Lincolnshire port had heard of John Clare and were interested in his poetry. On 15th October he wrote to John Taylor: '... the Mayor of the Town sent for me as soon as he heard I had come & treated me in a very hearty manner & wished me to procure him two copys of my whole poems & desired me to insert his name in every Vol. ...'[8] He was introduced to the literary circle of the town, and was received by the Mayor, who gave a dinner in the poet's honour – but Clare resolutely refused to make a speech.

On the evening following the Mayor's banquet, a group of young men wanted to take Clare off to another place for supper, where they wished him to make a speech especially for them. But as soon as he realised this, he declined their offer, assuring them that they would get little value for their money. He simply promised to sign and send the books he had been asked for as soon as he could get back to Helpston.

Unknown to the poet, the young men whose supper Clare had refused had made a collection and put £10 into his wallet. He did not find the gift until he returned home. The discovery moved him to tears of regret that he had been so unwilling to do anything for such kindness. With that gift and the profits from the sale of his books, Clare hoped that he would have enough money to see his family through the winter. But there were pressing debts to be settled; moreover, for the next three months he and his family suffered from a fen fever brought back from Boston – which lasted for about six weeks.

Having been unable to do any work for several months, and having incurred expenses for medical assistance, Clare found himself deeper than ever in debt, with scarcely any prospects of raising himself from his abject state of poverty. And so, on 3rd April, he wrote to John Taylor. After referring to his continued efforts to sell his books by means of advertisements in the *Stamford News*, he appended a doleful remark: '… if I succeed in selling them all well & good if not it will not be the first disappointment I have met with.'[9] He continued:

> & now my dear Taylor I will as a man of business say what I have long neglected as I never liked to refer to but it is a thi[ng tha]t must be & it will never interfere in our friendship be as it may – so I should like to know at your leisure how I stand with you in my accounts & my mind will be set at rest on that score at once for if there is anything coming to me it will be acceptable at any time & if there is nothing I shall be content the number printed of the three first vols I have known a long while by Drurys account … I hope you will not feel offended at my mentioning the matter as I do it for no other wish than to make us greater & better friends if possible[10]

At first Taylor refused to give Clare any accounts, and treated all payments as voluntary gifts. The firm of Taylor and Hessey was dissolved in 1825, but in August 1829, after much correspondence, Taylor finally submitted the accounts to Clare; however they were utterly confusing and he did little to explain their complexities.

The accounts were divided into five sections from *A* to *E*. *Account A* (the general account) recorded the various sums paid out to Clare between 1820 and 1829, showing the profits on sales and the dividends received. It was this account which claimed that Clare owed his publishers £140 – a figure he naturally disputed. *Account B* detailed the list of subscribers to the fund started by Lord Radstock. *Account C* covered the four editions of *Poems Descriptive of Rural Life and Scenery*. Although this account revealed that the book had sold successfully, to Clare's surprise it had made no profit at all for the poet. Taylor, Hessey and Drury had each received a share of the takings, with Taylor paying himself an extra five per cent for his work as editor. *Account D* was concerned with *The Village Minstrel*, which showed a profit of £58, half of which went to the publishers (including Drury) and half to the author. Set against this, however, was a fee of fifteen guineas for the portrait of Clare by William Hilton. But as Clare pointed out, this portrait was done for Taylor at his own request; he could not see why it should be charged to *The Village Minstrel* account. *Account E* told the sad story of *The Shepherd's Calendar*. Only 425 copies had been sold, and the account had an adverse balance of £60.

From these accounts, Clare discovered that £100 originally paid into the Subscription Fund by Taylor and Hessey had been paid back to the firm. There were several other items which Clare had to ask Taylor about. One was the payment promised for poems printed in the *London Magazine*, of which Taylor was editor. Another query was about £7 which James Hessey had received from a Duchess who wished to help the poet. The money had never been sent to him, nor was it shown in any of the accounts. Therefore, Clare argued, he was still owed at least £43. But Hessey had parted from Taylor, and was now bankrupt. Taylor argued that he could not be held responsible for the accounts of his ex-partner.[11]

Nothing appeared to be in Clare's favour. Others had profited from his work, but financially his own efforts went unrewarded. All this added up to a depressing sense of failure which led to a period of severe illness. His attempts at farming, mainly market gardening, though they did not bring much profit, did at least give him a feeling of self-dependence which he had never known before. He also became a frequent visitor to the Bishop's Palace in Peterborough where he was allowed the use of a room as a private study.

On 14th July 1830, during a stay at the Palace, he was taken by the Bishop and his wife to see a production of *The Merchant of Venice* at the local theatre, where he displayed (perhaps for the first time in public) his emotional instability. All went well for the first three acts, but when Portia rose to deliver judgement, Clare became so emotionally involved in the action that he suddenly rose from his seat and began cursing the actor who performed the part of Shylock. The audience was not used to such behaviour, and he was quickly escorted out of the theatre.

Clare returned to Helpston full of remorse and agitation. When the Reverend Charles Mossop saw him the following day, he was so alarmed at the poet's condition that he sought immediate medical help. As soon as Clare was well enough to write, he sent his apologies to Mrs Marsh, who in her reply readily forgave him for the embarrassment caused.

Clare's outburst at the theatre was the beginning of a long period of severe illnesses which were to culminate in his mental breakdown. By 1832 his farming had become unprofitable. Fortunately, Lord Fitzwilliam was sympathetic to his plight. He had recently built a cottage at Northborough, three miles from Helpston, and agreed to Clare being the first tenant at a rent of £15 a year. There was also two acres of land and an orchard. But despite this generosity Clare was reluctant to leave Helpston. It was hard for him to tear himself away from those favourite scenes of his childhood. It meant leaving more than a home. It meant leaving the trees and bushes, the birds and flowers he knew so well. Nothing could ever compensate for that lost world. As Edward Storey puts it, '[Clare] was severing himself physically and spiritually from a place which had known all his secrets, dreams, triumphs and despairs.'[12] His wealthy friends eventually persuaded him to move, and they gave him enough money to establish a smallholding. His patron Eliza Emmerson dubbed him 'Farmer John' and sent him £10 to buy a cow.

The strangeness of Clare's new home gave him, to begin with, much time for reflection, and within days of arriving he was at work on 'The Flitting':

> Ive left my own old home of homes
> Green fields and every pleasant place
> The summer like a stranger comes
> I pause and hardly know her face
> I miss the hazels happy green
> The blue bells quiet hanging blooms
> Where envys sneer was never seen
> Where staring malice never comes

He was forgetting the many harsh things he had said about the people of Helpston, where he had known plenty of envy and 'staring malice'. But it is not only the cottage or the village that he mourns:

> I sit me in my corner chair
> That seems to feel itself from home
> I hear bird music here and there
> From awthorn hedge and orchard come
> I hear but all is strange and new

Clare describes his feelings in a landscape in which nature is apparently no less benevolent than in Helpston – the trees are no less green, the birds still sing – but in which the scenes are strange, 'mere shadows', 'vague unpersonifying things', compared with his 'old haunts', rich in associations:

> Here every tree is strange to me
> All foreign where ere I go
> There's none where boyhood made a swee
> Or clambered up to rob a crow
> No hollow tree or woodland bower
> Well known when joy was beating high
> Where beauty ran to shun a shower
> And love took pains to keep her dry

For more than two hundred lines Clare laments the world he has lost, and he clings desperately to those things he has managed to salvage – his memory, his books, his love for nature's simple pleasures, such as the daisies, birds' nests, and 'a love for every single weed'.

Towards the end of the poem he begins to argue himself out of this nostalgia and to accept his new situation, by trying to attach his associations of Helpston to the trees and flowers around him in Northborough. He is attempting to replace his old love of nature as it was in Helpston, and not elsewhere, with a love of nature as it is everywhere. So 'The Flitting' ends on a positive note:

> Time looks on pomp with careless moods
> Or killing apathys disdain
> – So where old marble citys stood
> Poor persecuted weeds remain
> She feels a love for little things
> That very few can feel beside
> And still the grass eternal springs
> Where castles stood and grandeur died[13]

NOTES

1. British Museum: *Egerton Folios*, 2245-48 – 21 January 1820
2. *Ibid.* 1 August 1823
3. Mark Storey (ed.): *The Letters of John Clare*, page 349
4. Mark Storey (ed.): *Clare: The Critical Heritage*, page 201
5. *Ibid.* page 205
6. *Ibid.* page 206-207
7. Mark Storey (ed.): *The Letters of John Clare*, page 415
8. *Ibid.* page 440
9. *Ibid.* page 425
10. *Ibid.*
11. For a fuller account of Clare's financial affairs, see J.W. and Anne Tibble: *John Clare: A Life*, pages 310ff. For the correspondence between Clare and his publishers on these matters, see Mark Storey (ed.): *The Letters of John Clare*, pages 474-485 and 685-690.
12. Edward Storey: *A Right to Song*, page 232
13. *The Oxford Authors: John Clare*, page 250

CHAPTER 8

The Clouded Mind

For several years Clare had been planning to publish another collection of poems at his own expense. On 1st September 1832 he received from a Peterborough printer one hundred copies of his proposals for the publication of a volume of cottage poems under the title *The Midsummer Cushion*. He had publicly announced it in the *Athenaeum* in August, and drafted his introduction and explanation of the book's title: 'It is a very old custom among villagers in summer time to stick a piece of greensward full of field flowers & place it as an ornament in their cottages which ornaments are called Midsummer Cushions.'[1] This was his letter to the subscribers:

> The proposals for publishing these fugitives being addressed to friends, no further apology is necessary than the statement of facts. The truth is that difficulty has grown up like a tree of the forest, and being no longer able to conceal it I meet it in the best way possible by attempting to publish these for my own benefit and that of a large family
>
> It were false delicacy to make an idle parade of independence in my situation; and it would be unmanly to make a troublesome appeal to persons public or like a public petitioner

> Friends neither expect this from me nor wish me to do it to others, though it is partly owing to such advice that I have been induced to come forward with these proposals, and if they are successful they will render me a benefit, and if not they will not cancel any obligations I may have received from my friends, public or private, to whom my best wishes are due; and having said this much in furtherance of my intentions I will conclude by explaining them[2]

The book was to be printed 'on fine paper, and published as soon as a sufficent number of subscribers are produced to defray the expenses of publishing ... The price will not exceed seven shillings and six pence.'[3] These proposals were distributed among Clare's friends and acquaintances, and by the end of October he had a list of two hundred subscribers.

Outwardly all looked promising, and there was good reason to hope that Clare's reputation as a poet would be re-established. But when the Peterborough printer, who had agreed to publish the volume, said he wanted £100 for the steel engravings, Clare had second thoughts. He did not have that amount of money and thought he must abandon the project.

Eliza Emmerson, however, had been negotiating with How and Whittaker of Peterborough, who agreed to take over the publication on the security of Clare's two hundred subscribers. She advised him to sell the copyright of this new volume for an immediate sum of £40, but his hopes of seeing *The Midsummer Cushion* published in full and under that title were soon shattered. Some of the contents were selected by Mrs Emmerson, modified, edited and 'cleaned up' by other hands to form *The Rural Muse,* a title not chosen by Clare. More than half of *The Midsummer Cushion* was left unpublished until 1979.

The Rural Muse was published by How and Whittaker in 1835. It was dedicated to Lord Fitzwilliam and bore, as a frontispiece, an engraving of Clare's cottage, with one of Northborough Church on the title page. But, according to Frederick Martin, the publishers had been 'fearful of risking money in printing too large a quantity of rural verse, so much out of fashion for the time.'[4] Their fears may have been justified; *The Rural Muse* did not sell well. In his *Biographical Sketches of Remarkable People*, Spencer T. Hall said that he 'could have bought any number of the neat, uncut volumes, at a bookseller's shop in Stamford, in 1849, at only eighteen pence a copy.'[5]

The failure to publish *The Midsummer Cushion*, and the poor response to *The Rural Muse*, meant the end of the road for Clare's ambitions. Around this time, anxieties over his future as a poet, and a growing sense of failure and deepening financial crisis reulted in really serious attacks of psychosomatic ailments. In September 1830 he wrote to Taylor:

> I have not been able until now to write to you – for I have been dreadfully ill – & I can scarcely manage even now to muster courage sufficient to feel myself able to [make out] write a letter but you will excuse all – I have been bled blistered and cupped & have now a seaton in my neck & tho much better I have made many fears as to recovery but I keep my mind as quiet as I can – and am able to read a Newspaper – all I regret is that I cannot describe my feelings sufficiently to benefit from our friend Dr Darlings kind advice in whom I always had the greatest confidence – my fancys & feelings vary very often but I now feel a great numbness in my right shoulder[6]

In the same letter he told Taylor of the addition to his family of another daughter (Sophia), born on 24th July 1830.

In 1831 he wrote: '... my future prospects seem to be no sleep – a general debility – a stupid & stunning apathy or lingering madness & death – my dreads are very apprehensive & uneasy.'[7] It is very difficult to tell with any certainty when Clare's mental instability actually began. His mental and physical disorders were closely connected, and it seems fairly certain that his mind had begun to be affected long before he suffered his first attack of insanity in 1830.

We may suspect, indeed, that there had always been something in his manner or conversation that suggested abnormality. He was always 'itching after rhyme' – a compulsion so strong that at times it controlled him and drove him to write for several days continuously. He wrote when he was hungry and weary, when the world discouraged and mocked him, when his hopes of the immortality that he so much desired for his poetry were almost dead. Those who knew him had prophesied, when he was only a boy, that he would lose his reason.

As he grew older, he became very susceptible to alcohol. In January 1820 Edward Drury had written to John Taylor:

> It is to be feared that [Clare] will be afflicted with insanity if his talent continues to be forced as it has been these 4 months past; he has no other mode of easing the fever that oppresses him after a tremendous fit of rhyming except by getting tipsy. A simple pint of ale very often does this, and next morning a stupor with headache and pains across the chest afflicts him very severely. Then he is melancholy and completely hypochondriac – you will easily suppose how true is my account when I assure you he has rhymed and

> written for 3 days and 3 nights without hardly eating or sleeping.[8]

In the winter of 1821, or early in 1822, Clare, in the anxiety and disappointments of his struggles, had exhausted himself in composing 'The Dream'. He wrote afterwards: 'I mustnt do no more terrible things yet … they stir me up to such a pitch that leaves a disrelish for my old accustomed wanderings after nature'; and he called his Muse a 'fickle Hussey' who 'sometimes stilts me up to madness & then leaves me as a beggar by the way side with no more life [than] whats mortal & that nearly extinguished by mellancholy forbodings.'[9]

During the autumn and winter of 1831-32 Clare's health was poor, and he was often troubled by severe depression and fear. At Christmas he made a list of the presents that he had promised the children – books for them all, with 'Dame Trott and her Cat' and 'The House that Jack Built' for John and Sophy, the two youngest; for he said that these little books often gave him 'more pleasure and more knowledge than many that are written for men.'[10]

On 4th January 1833 Patty gave birth to another son (Charles). Clare had yet another life dependent on him, when he could not support those that he had already. Morbidly anxious, he wrote to Dr Darling, describing symptoms, which, among other things, seem to have included some kind of sleep disorder:

> … sound affects me very much & things evil as well [as] good thoughts are continually rising in my mind … I cannot sleep for I am asleep as it were with my eyes open & I fear chills come over me & a sort of nightmare awake … I cannot keep my mind right as it were for I wish to read

> and cannot – there is a sort of numbing through my private parts which I cannot describe & when I was so indisposed last winter I felt as if I had circulation in the blood & at times as if it went round me & at other times such a sinking as if I was going to sink through the bed ... I fear I shall get worse & worse ere you write to me for I have been out for a walk & can scarcely bear up against my fancys or feelings[11]

In the winter of 1835-36 Clare's mental condition was very disturbed. 'His ordinarily quiet behaviour gave way at times to fits of excitement, during which he would talk in a violent manner to those around him.'[12] To make matters worse, his mother died on 18th December 1835 at the age of 78. He was deeply upset and his Christmas was made miserable by her loss. His father, now totally crippled and in need of care, left Helpston and went to live with him at Northborough, thereby adding another burden to the already overworked Patty.

In the late autumn of 1836 John Taylor was in Retford; on his way back to London at the beginning of December he visited Clare at Northborough. Having heard of the poet's poor health and increasingly strange behaviour, he thought it wise to take a local doctor with him. Taylor's account of the visit makes sad reading:

> The following morning at seven I set off to see Clare in a chaise accompanied by a medical gentleman of Stamford, who was to give me his opinion respecting Clare's health. We found him sitting in a chimney corner looking much as usual. He talked properly to me in reply to all my questions, knew all the people of whom I spoke, and smiled

> at my reminding him of the events of past days. But his mind is sadly enfeebled. He is constantly speaking to himself and when I listened I heard such words as these, pronounced a great many times over and over with great rapidity – 'God bless them all', 'Keep them from evil', 'Doctors'. But who it was of whom he spoke I could not tell – whether his children, or doctors, or everybody. But I think the latter. His children, seven in number, are a very fine family, strongly resembling him; the youngest, a boy of three or four years old; the eldest, a girl, sixteen. There are three boys and four girls. The medical man's opinion was that Clare should go to some asylum. His wife is a very clever, active woman, and keeps them all very respectable and comfortable, but she cannot manage to control her husband at times; he is very violent, I dare say, occasionally. His old father is still living with them. We went thence to see a clergyman who had been always kind to Clare for twenty years, and has promised to see Earl Fitzwilliam about an asylum.[13]

Lunatic asylums in the mid-nineteenth century were generally appalling places for people to spend the rest of their lives. Fortunately Clare's London friends found a private home where he could receive specialised medical care. And so, on 13th June 1837, Taylor wrote a note which he sent down with a man who travelled from London to fetch Clare: 'It is my sincere hope that the Medical Care which is provided for you near this place will be effectual to your recovery. The Bearer will bring you up to Town and take every care of you on the road.'[14]

John Clare was escorted to High Beach, a private asylum in Epping Forest, run on progressive principles, not unlike modern therapy, by Dr Matthew Allen. Allen's method was to allow his patients the maximum amount of freedom, to encourage them to occupy themselves with healthy work and recreation, and to establish between them and their attendants a relationship of complete confidence and friendship; he believed that, if the patient was treated with honesty and compassion, he would give his trust in return, and that would enable the doctor to treat him effectively.

Clare arrived at High Beach, according to Dr Allen, 'exceedingly miserable, every instant bemoaning his poverty, and his mind did not appear so much lost and deranged as suspended in its movements by the oppressive and permanent state of anxiety, and fear, and vexation, produced by the excitement of excessive flattery at one time, and neglect at another, his extreme poverty and over exertion of body and mind.'[15]

The patients were kept under no more restraint than was absolutely necessary for their own safety and that of others. Clare was encouraged to write whenever he felt like it and, although a certain watchfulness was probably exercised, he was permitted to wander in the grounds or the forest – in fact to lead a life as much as possible like his old one, but without its attendant worries.

After an initial period of depression, Clare appears to have responded well to the treatment he received at High Beach. By December 1839 Dr Allen was able to write to John Taylor: 'I am happy in having it in my power to say that our friend is improved and improving – in appearance wonderfully – stout and rosy,' even to the extent of saying that Clare's lot now was 'all life and fun'.[16]

It was hardly that! Feeling alone, severed from love, friends and family, he viewed the asylum as a prison, a 'hell of a madhouse', resembling 'a slave ship from Africa'. Everywhere he met deception, surrounded, he thought, by 'mock friends and real enemies'. In his disturbed frame of mind he was quite unable to understand why he was so situated. He suffered delusions, believing himself at different times to be Ben Caunt, a well known prize fighter, Lord Byron, Robert Burns, and various other people, while also maintaining a fantasy that he had two wives – his adolescent childhood sweetheart Mary Joyce and his legal wife Patty. He was convinced that he was already married to Mary when he had to marry Patty; that Patty came into his life solely to bear his children when he was not really free to marry her, and that his 'imprisonment' at High Beach – actually a voluntary confinement – was punishment for his 'bigamy'.

There is little sign that Clare was suicidal or dangerous. Matthew Allen believed that his illness was due to financial insecurity, with a wife and seven children to support. He was certain that if a small pension could have been obtained then for Clare 'he would have recovered instantly and most probably remained well for life.'[17] But no amount of money could save Clare now. His needs could not be met by anything that charity or pity could provide. The sickness had been there longer than anyone realized. It was a poverty of the heart now; he was very homesick, and longing to be reunited with Mary.

On 17th June 1840, a report of Clare's death, previously published in the *Halifax Express*, appeared in *The Times*. Dr Allen wrote immediately to the London paper to correct the statement and to appeal for subscriptions to help Clare and his family. His contradiction of the facts, with his own account of his patient's health, was published on 23rd June:

> [John Clare] is at present in excellent health and looks very well, and is in mind, though full of many strange delusions,

> in a much more comfortable and happy state than he was when he first came ... the moment he gets pen or pencil in hand he begins to write most beautiful poetic effusions. Yet he has never been able to maintain in conversation, nor even in writing prose, the appearance of sanity for two minutes or two lines together, and yet there is no indication of insanity in any of his poetry.'

Although Clare was 'in excellent health', no moves seem to have been taken towards his release. His sponsors presumably feared that his return to family responsibilities would mean renewal of the pressures that led to his mental breakdown. He would, they thought, be better off at High Beach. Visitors often came to see him; one, the journalist Cyrus Redding, published an account of his visit in the *English Journal* for May 1841. He was accompanied by a friend who had known Clare previously. They found the poet hoeing in a field near the house, and called him away from his work to talk to him. Redding's companion was surprised to see how much Clare's appearance had changed, for he had put on weight and was no longer pale and attenuated as he had once been:

> We found a little man of muscular frame and firmly set, his complexion fresh and forehead high, a nose somewhat aquiline, and a long full chin. The expression of his countenance was more pleasing but somehow less intellectual than that in the engraved portrait prefixed to his works in the edition of 'The Village Minstrel', published in 1821 ... He made some remarks illustrative of the difference between the aspect of the country at High Beach and that of the fens from whence he had come –

> alluded to Northborough and Peterborough – and spoke of the loneliness away from his wife, expressing a great desire to go home, and to have the society of women.[18]

Clare spent just over four years at High Beach, but his mental condition showed little change. In July 1841, desperately unhappy, he escaped. It took him four days to walk the eighty miles back to his cottage at Northborough.

His account of this extraordinary passage, entitled 'Journey out of Essex', is one of the most pitiful ever told. It begins: 'July 18 – 1841 – Felt very melancholly …,' and recounts how his removal was inspired by some gypsies in the forest. One of them offered to assist in his 'escape from the mad house' by hiding him in their camp.[19] When he returned the following day they had gone, but he decided to follow the route they had suggested.

And so, on 20th July – eluding the keepers or attendants whose duty it was to watch the patients unobtrusively on their forest walks – with nothing more than 'honest courage' and a little tobacco, he set out on the long journey, determined to find Mary, whom he believed was waiting for him. But, not having made a note of the gypsies' directions, he took the wrong turning, lost his way, and soon found he was heading south instead of north. When he reached a public house he asked for directions to Enfield:

> I walked down the lane gently and was soon in Enfield Town and bye and bye on the great York Road where it was all plain sailing and steering ahead meeting no enemy and fearing none I reached Stevenage where being Night I got over a gate crossed over the corner of a green paddock where seeing a pond or hollow in the corner I [was] forced to stay of a respectable distance to keep from falling into

> it for my legs were nearly knocked up and began to stagger I scaled some old rotten paleings into the yard and then had higher pailings to clamber over to get into the shed or hovel which I did with difficulty being rather weak and to my good luck I found some trusses of clover piled up about 8 or more feet square which I gladly mounted and slept on there was some trays in the hovel on which I could have reposed had I not found a better bed I slept soundly but had a very uneasy dream I thought my first wife [Mary] lay on my arm and somebody took her away from my side which made me wake up rather unhappy ... I thought as I awoke somebody said 'Mary' but nobody was near – I lay down with my head towards the north to show my self the steering point in the morning[20]

Cold and exhausted, on the third day he satisfied his hunger by eating grass at the roadside. By the time he reached Stilton, he could hardly walk; but on reaching the inn at Norman Cross, he asked if the road to the right led to Peterborough, and was told that it did:

> as soon as ever I was on it I found myself in homes way and went on rather more cheerfull though I [was] forced to rest oftener than usual before I got to Peterborough a man and woman passed me in a cart and on hailing me as they passed I found they were neighbours from Helpston where I used to live – I told them I was knocked up which they could easily see and that I had neither eat nor drank any thing since I left Essex when I told my story they clubbed together and threw me fivepence out of the cart I picked it up and called at a small public house near the

bridge where I had two half pints of ale and twopenn'oth of bread and cheese when I had started quite refreshed only my feet was more crippled than ever and I could scarcely make a walk of it over the stones and being half ashamed to sit down in the street I forced to keep on the move and got through Peterborough better than I expected when I got on the high road I rested on the stone heaps as I passed till I was able to go on afresh and bye and bye I passed Walton and soon reached Werrington ... when a cart met me with a man and a woman and a boy in it when nearing me the woman jumped out and caught hold of my hands and wished me to get into the cart but I refused and thought her either drunk or mad but when I was told it was my second wife Patty I got in and was soon at Northborough but Mary was not there neither could I get any information about her further than the old story of her being dead six years ago which might be taken from a bran new old Newspaper printed a dozen years ago but I took no notice of the blarney having seen her myself about a twelvemonth ago alive and well as young as ever – so here I am homeless at home[21]

The last words of this tragic account are:

July 24th 1841 Returned home out of Essex and found no Mary – her and her family are as nothing to me now though she herself was once the dearest of all – and how can I forget[22]

Three days later he wrote a letter to Mary Joyce, whom he now addressed as 'Mary Clare – Glinton':

My dear wife

I have written an account of my journey or rather escape from Essex for your amusement & hope it may divert your leisure hours – I would have told you before now that I got here to Northborough last friday night but not being able to see you or hear where you was I soon began to feel homeless at home & shall bye & bye feel nearly hopeless but not so lonely as I did in Essex – for I can see Glinton church & feeling that Mary is safe if not happy & I am gratified though my home is no home to me my hopes are not entirely hopeless while even the memory of Mary lives so near me God bless you My dear Mary Give my love to your dear & beautiful family & to your Mother – & believe me as I ever have been & shall be My dearest Mary

your affectionate Husband
John Clare[23]

Throughout the autumn Clare wrote many poems and fragmentary verses, most of them containing thoughts of Mary, 'the muse of every song I write'. In some, he expressed his loneliness and the hopelessness of searching for her whom he could not find:

I've wandered many a weary mile
Love in my heart was burning
To seek a home in Mary[s] smile
But cold is loves returning
The cold ground was a feather bed
Truth never acts contrary
I had no home above my head
My home was love and Mary[24]

Clare refused to accept the fact that Mary Joyce had died on 16th July 1838.

NOTES

1. See introductory note in *John Clare: The Midsummer Cushion,* ed. Kelsey Thornton and Anne Tibble
2. J.W. and Anne Tibble: *John Clare: A Life,* page 314
3. See Introduction to *The Midsummer Cushion*
4. Frederick Martin: *The Life of John Clare,* page 260
5. Mark Storey (ed.): *Clare: The Critical Heritage,* page 279
6. Mark Storey (ed.): *The Letters of John Clare,* page 513
7. *Ibid.* page 537
8. Mark Storey (ed.): *Clare: The Critical Heritage,* page 33
9. Mark Storey (ed.): *The Letters of John Clare,* page 230
10. J.W. and Anne Tibble: *John Clare: A Life,* page 318
11. Mark Storey (ed.): *The Letters of John Clare,* page 615
12. Frederick Martin: *The Life of John Clare,* page 254
13. J.W. and Anne Tibble: *John Clare: A Life,* page 330
14. Quoted by June Wilson in *Green Shadows: The Life of John Clare,* page 229
15. See Geoffrey Grigson's Introduction to *Poems of John Clare's Madness,* page 6
16. See J.W. and Anne Tibble: *John Clare: A Life,* page 339
17. Grigson: *Op. cit.*
18. Mark Storey (ed.): *Clare: The Critical Heritage,* page 248
19. *John Clare by Himself,* page 257
20. *Ibid.* page 258
21. *Ibid.* page 264
22. *Ibid.* page 265
23. Mark Storey (ed.): *The Letters of John Clare,* page 649
24. *The Oxford Authors: John Clare,* page 281

CHAPTER 9

The Last Years

For five months – July to December 1841 – John Clare lived 'homeless at home', as he put it, at Northborough. The Reverend Charles Mossop, who had known him since his earliest days as a poet, visited the Clare household and found the situation strained. Although Patty did her best to keep her husband quietly occupied, by Christmas she had become alarmed by his behaviour. He had turned violent, and between bouts of terrible temper and depression he would sit in a corner muttering to himself. Patty was afraid of what might happen next, afraid for her children.

Mossop had already suggested that Clare should go to the new asylum at Northampton, if it were decided that he should require treatment. And now, on the advice of Lord Fitzwilliam, Clare was seen by Dr Fenwick Skrimshire and Dr William Page. Both doctors confirmed that he was 'in a state of lunacy'; on 29th December he was taken from his home and entered as a patient at the Northampton General Lunatic Asylum.

Frederick Martin maintained – and we can well believe it – that Clare 'struggled hard when the keepers came to fetch him, imploring them, with tears in his eyes, to leave him at his little cottage, and seeing all resistance useless, declaring his intention to die rather than to go to such another prison as that from which he had escaped.'[1] But the struggle was in vain. Patty herself wept bitterly as her husband was removed and driven away to the asylum. He had seen the last of his home and his wife; from Northampton there would be no escape.

The certificate for his confinement stated that the patient was forty-nine, that his usual employment was gardening, that he had been married for twenty-two years, and had seven children. As was customary in certificates of insanity at that time, it was stated that Clare's problems were 'hereditary', although there was no evidence of insanity in his family. The certificate also stated that the patient had had several attacks, the first symptoms having been apparent fourteen years earlier, and that indications of the existing attack had been noticed four years ago. The information that he had 'escaped' from High Beach was twice underlined, and the answers to the questions as to whether 'he had ever attempted or threatened violence to self or others', and whether he was 'idiotic, mischievous or dirty', were both 'No'. To the question whether insanity had been preceded by 'any severe or continued mental emotion or exertion', Dr Skrimshire wrote: 'After years addicted to Poetical prosings.'[2] The diagnosis was of course sheer quackery, though Clare was undeniably ill, and quite beyond the care of his family.

Though one might perhaps think nineteenth century asylums likely to be rather grim institutions, Clare was in many ways well cared for at both those in which he lived. This was, however, partly due to preferential treatment. Though admitted as a pauper patient, Clare was supported financially by Lord Fitzwilliam, whose family was one of the richest estate owners in the country. His generosity allowed Clare to enjoy some of the privileges of being a private patient (he had, for example, a room of his own).

The Northampton General Lunatic Asylum had been opened

on 1st August 1838. It was a large establishment, 'containing, on the average, some four hundred patients, the great majority of them paupers. The private patients have to themselves a large sitting-room, somewhat similar to a gentleman's library, the windows of which overlook the front garden, the valley of the Nene and the town of Northampton.'[3] The asylum was enlarged in 1843, and the total cost (including twenty-four acres of land owned by the Fitzwilliam family) amounted to £35,000. When Clare became a patient in 1841 it was, therefore, a new building with new staff, new ideas and a degree of comfort far removed from the older mental asylums. Its staff was engaged to pursue the new policies of treating the insane like normal human beings in need of care, peace and rest. Nevertheless, Clare's own attitude was that he was in prison.

The Superintendent of the asylum was Dr Thomas Pritchard. He was a man of strong character who, like Dr Allen, believed that better results could be obtained not by locking the patients away but by treating them with kindness and sympathy. Dr Pritchard classified Clare as 'harmless', and in the early years he was allowed to wander the surrounding countryside and town at will, returning only for meals and bed. His favourite spot was the portico of All Saints Church, where he would sit for hours. The people of Northampton were invariably kind to him, and it was not unusual for him to receive some little gift of tobacco or ale. The local artist George Maine drew the poet sitting there, looking well dressed, well fed, and with note book and pencil in hand, and in 1844 Clare's portrait was painted by another local artist, Thomas Grimshaw. (See illustration)

Dr Pritchard left the asylum in 1845, and his place was taken by Dr P.R. Nesbitt, who had a great admiration for Clare's poetry and took a keen interest in him. He felt, however, that various people in the town had shown mistaken kindness in giving ale to the poet, as it was 'injurious in its effects'. He was, therefore, no longer allowed to wander alone outside the asylum grounds.

Clare remained at the Northampton asylum for the last twenty-three years of his life. He received a number of visitors, but he sometimes believed he had never been visited or was abandoned; perhaps he did not always recognise his visitors or forgot they had been to see him. His sons John and William came occasionally, and Charles often wrote to him; but he worked for a solicitor and probably found it difficult to make the journey from Northborough to Northampton. He died in 1852 at the age of 19. There is no record that Patty ever visited her husband; it is quite likely that she was advised not to do so because her presence would distress him. In any case, she was often ill herself and could not afford to make the expensive journey to Northampton.

In June 1847 Clare wrote to his son Charles: '... I must [say] that Frederick & John had better not come unless they wish to do so for it is a bad Place & I have fears that they may get trapped as prisoners as I hear some have been & I may not see them or even hear they have been here.'[4] He did not realise that his eldest son (Frederick) had been dead for nearly four years, and that his daughter Anna had also died. Parker Clare had died in March 1846 at the age of 82; but, if he was ever told of these deaths, his son had obviously forgotten and believed that they were still living in the cottage at Northborough.

The routine of life at the asylum continued unbroken. Clare's physical health continued to improve, but his state of mind veered between severe depression and a tranquil resignation. One distinctive symptom of his insanity, both at High Beach and later at Northampton, was his intermittent delusion that he was other people. G.J. de Wilde, editor of the *Northampton Mercury*, recalled a meeting with him when, not knowing the poet, he was startled to hear Clare claim as his own some lines from Byron and Shakespeare:

> 'Yours!' I exclaimed. 'Who are you? These are Byron's and Shakespeare's verses, not yours!' 'It's all the same,' he answered, changing a quid from one cheek to the other. 'I'm John Clare now. I was Byron and Shakespeare formerly. At different times you know I'm different people – that is the same person with different names.' And then he went on to identify himself with a most miscellaneous and unselect lot of celebrities – great warriors, prize frighters, and some eminent blackguards.[5]

Clare's adopted identities, as de Wilde noted, were remarkably varied, ranging from the boxers Ben Caunt, Jack Randall and Tom Spring, through Lord Nelson and the Duke of Wellington to Robert Burns, Lord Byron and Shakespeare. The question of his identity troubled Clare deeply, not so much because he confused himself with other people, but because he had some idea that the whole world was united in a vast conspiracy to make him forget himself. 'Perhaps,' writes June Wilson, 'it was an echo from the years when he had been deeply wounded to find himself cast aside by a public who had been entertained for a brief season by the novelty of a peasant poet.'[6]

Before his removal to Northampton, Clare had written in his notebook: 'A very good common place counsel is *Self Identity* to bid our hearts not to forget our own selves and always to keep self in the first place lest all the world who always keeps us behind it should forget us all together – forget not thyself and the world will not forget thee – forget thyself and the world will willingly forget thee till thou art nothing but a living-dead man dwelling among shadows and falsehood ... But I cannot forget that I'm a man and it would be dishonest and unmanly in me to do so ... I am often troubled at times to know that should the world have the impudence not to know me but willingly forget me whether any single individual would be honest enough to know me – such people would be usefull as the knocker to a door or the bell of a cryer to own the dead alive or the lost found.'[7]

Over the years Clare continued to write, and in this respect he benefited from the appointment in April 1845 of William Knight as House Steward to the asylum. He took a keen interest in Clare, befriended him, and encouraged his creativity. He also began the task of transcribing into two large volumes over eight hundred poems written at High Beach and Northampton. They were copied from manuscripts presented to him by the author. When Knight moved to Birmingham in 1850 the work was continued by other (unknown) copyists. These manuscripts are now housed in the Local Studies Collection at Northampton Central Library.

The poems written during the asylum years are exceptionally fine. Two major undertakings of this period were *Child Harold* and *Don Juan*. Clare used Byron as his 'persona': the inviolate aristocrat and satirist, untroubled by the sexual guilt and social inferiority which ravaged Clare himself. *Child Harold* bears amazing witness to Clare's determination to establish meaning and purpose in his life:

> Fame blazed upon me like a comets glare
> Fame waned and left me like a fallen star
> Because I told the evil what they are

And truth and falsehood never wished to mar
My Life hath been a wreck – and Ive gone far
For peace and truth – and hope – for home and rest
– Like Edens gates – fate throws a constant bar –
Thoughts may o'ertake the sunset in the west
– Man meets no home within a womans breast[8]

The majority of Clare's poems written during this period, however, are love poems, and they speak of youth and happiness; their melody is as joyous and spontaneous as birds singing in the spring, and there is a sense of liberation in them, as though the poet had come through the horrors of darkness out into the dew-laden freshness of a spring morning.

'Tis spring my love 'tis spring
And the birds begin to sing
If 'twas winter left alone with you
Your happy form and face
Would make a sunny place
And prove a finer flower then ever grew

'Tis spring my love 'tis spring
On the hazels catkins hing
And the snowdrop wi' blebs o' dew
Is not more white within
Then your bosom's hidden skin
The sweetest bonny flower that ever grew[9]

Other poems, produced in moods of sorrow and depression, are particularly moving. In 'I Am', perhaps the best known of them, he wrestled once more with the problem of self-identity, his loneliness and isolation:

I am – yet what I am, none cares or knows;
   My friends forsake me like a memory lost:–
I am the self-consumer of my woes;
   They rise and vanish in oblivion's host
Like shadows in love's frenzied stifled throes:–
And yet I am, and live – like vapours tost

Into the nothingness of scorn and noise, –
   Into the living sea of waking dreams,
Where there is neither sense of life or joys,
   But the vast shipwreck of my life's esteems;
Even the dearest, that I love the best
Are strange – nay, rather stranger than the rest.

I long for scenes, where man hath never trod
   A place where women never smiled or wept
There to abide with my Creator, God;
   And sleep as I in childhood, sweetly slept
Untroubling, and untroubled where I lie,
The grass below – above the vaulted sky[10]

Much of Clare's poetry from this period reveals, in the calmest and most delicate manner, his injured feelings at what he believed to be his unjust 'imprisonment' and the neglect of his friends; sometimes he reveals with deep sighs and a completely broken heart his past happiness, and speaks most passionately about nature and love. He also makes his love and thirst for freedom movingly manifest. In a letter addressed to Dr Matthew Allen (written just after his 'escape' from High Beach) he confessed:

> I can be miserably happy in any situation & any place & could have staid in yours on the forest if any of my friends had noticed me or come to see me – but the greatest annoyance in such places as yours are those servants styld keepers who often assumed as much authority over me as if I had been their prisoner & not liking to quarrel I put up with it till I was weary of the place altogether so I heard the voice of freedom & started ...[11]

As the years went by, Clare's movements had to be more and more restricted. He went through bad periods when he became abusive and obscene or violent, and he would have been a danger outside not only to himself but to other people. But no matter how sympathetic and accommodating Dr Thomas Pritchard and his successors could be, Clare's troubled mind could only see himself as a helpless captive, as we read in a letter to his wife, dated 19th July 1848:

> I am in the land of sodom where all the peoples brains are turned the wrong way ... I write this in a green meadow by the side of the river agen Stokes Mill & I see three of your daughters & a son now and then the confusion & roar of Mill dams & locks is sounding very pleasant while I write & its a very beautiful Evening the meadows are greener than usual after the shower & the Rivers are brimful I think it is about two years since I was first sent up in this hell & not allowed to go out of the gates there never was a more disgraceful deception than this place it is the purgatorial hell & French Bastille of English liberty ...[12]

Deprived of the freedom to roam the fields or talk to people in the town, Clare felt there was nothing more for him to write about. 1848-50 was a particularly dry period. When it was suggested to him that he might write, he would say that he had forgotten how. But in the spring of 1850 he was persuaded to take up his pen again and wrote a few sonnets, including 'An Address to John Clare':

Well honest John how fare you now at home
The spring is come and birds are building nests
The old cock robin to the stye is come
With olive feathers and its ruddy breast
And the old cock with wattles and red comb
Struts with the hens and seems to like some best
Then crows and looks about for little crumbs
Swept out bye little folks an hour ago
The pigs sleep in the sty the bookman comes
The little boy lets home-close nesting go
And pockets tops and tawes where daiseys bloom
To look at the new number just laid down
With lots of pictures and good stories too
And Jack the jiant killers high renown[13]

In 1858 Dr Edwin Wing became superintendent of the asylum, and in March 1860 James Hipkins of Westminster wrote to him enquiring about Clare. Dr Wing replied, noting that his patient was 'very feeble in mind and still the subject of many mental delusions',[14] but he managed to persuade him to write a short letter to be enclosed with his. This was Clare's last letter, dated 8th March 1860:

Dear Sir

I am in a Madhouse & quite forget your Name or who you are you must excuse me for I have nothing to communicate or tell of & why I am shut up I dont know I have nothing to say so I conclude

Yours respectfully
John Clare[15]

During the next few years, Clare's mind became gradually more impaired and his physical strength declined. The inmates of the asylum treated him with the greatest respect – far greater than that previously allotted to him by the world outside. To his fellow sufferers he was always John Clare the poet, never Clare the farm labourer. Giving little utterance to his thoughts or dreams, and only smiling upon his companions now and then, he became confused and apathetic, and could only rarely delight in flowers and sunshine. In the winter of 1863-64 he wrote his last poem, 'Birds Nests':

Tis Spring warm glows the South
Chaffinchs carry the moss in his mouth
To the filbert hedges all day long
And charms the poet with his beautiful song
The wind blows blea oer the sedgey fen
But warm the sunshines by the little wood
Where the old Cow at her leisure chews her cud[16]

For the next few months Clare grew steadily weaker; he had to be put in a wheelchair when he went out in the asylum grounds. Several times he said, 'I want to go home' and, 'I have lived too long.' On Good Friday 1864 he ventured out for the last time, and on 10th May he had a paralytic seizure. He lived on for ten days, and then died quietly on the afternoon of 20th May, within two months of his seventy-first birthday.

It had always been his wish that he should be buried in his native village of Helpston. Instructions for his tomb appear in his 'Journal':

> I wish to lye on the North side of the Church yard just about the middle of the ground w[h]ere the Morning and Evening Sun can linger the longest on my Grave I wish to have a rough unhewn stone somthing in the form of a mile Stone so that the playing boys may not break it in their heedless pastimes with nothing more on it than this Inscription
> HERE Rest the HOPES and Ashes of JOHN CLARE
> I desire that no date be inserted there on as I wish it to live or dye with my poems and other writings which if they have merit with posterity it will and if they have not it is not worth preserving[17]

Plans had been made by the asylum authorities to bury him in a pauper's grave at nearby St Sepulchre's. But with the help of the Bellairs family, who had employed him when young, his body was returned by train, the following Tuesday, to his beloved Helpston. It arrived too late for burial on 24th May and so the coffin was placed on trestles in the bar of the Exeter Arms. There were rumours that it was not John Clare inside it at all, that the asylum could have sent any old lunatic to be buried in the village, and so the anxious villagers removed the lid of the coffin to witness for themselves the body of their local poet. There was even a rumour that a famous London surgeon wanted to dissect the brain to learn how a peasant could write poetry, and so the locals stood guard over the body until it could be buried the next day.

John Clare was buried in St Botolph's churchyard on Wednesday 25th May. Patty, her sons William and John, her daughter Eliza and Clare's sister Sophy were present, and so were the Reverend Charles Mossop and a few other friends. The inscription which Clare had desired was not put upon his tombstone, but a simple rectangular pitch-pointed slab bears the words:

SACRED TO THE MEMORY OF

JOHN CLARE

THE NORTHAMPTONSHIRE PEASANT POET

BORN JULY 13 1793 DIED MAY 20 1864

'A POET IS BORN NOT MADE'

Eight days after his death *The Northamptonshire Mercury* published a tribute by John Askham, a fellow poet from Wellingborough:

> It was with mingled feelings of sorrow and pleasure that I read in last week's *Mercury* the announcement of the death of John Clare, the peasant poet of our county. Sorrow to think that for so many years his bright intellect should have been overclouded with the awful shadow of insanity, and a melancholy pleasure to think that at last his long night of sorrow and disease was ended in death. I have always been an admirer of Clare's poetry; there is truthfulness and sincerity in it that wins upon the reader

> as he peruses his verse. He was perhaps the most natural poet that ever wrote, and certainly one of the most original … He uses none of the hackneyed phrases of mere rhymesters for effect, in all his verse … He is almost purely a descriptive poet; a true painter of nature in all her varied moods … What he might have done had his reason been spared of course is mere conjecture, but what he *has* done is a rich addition to our poetic literature.[18]

Within six weeks of Clare's death, John Taylor died on 5th July after a long illness. Eliza Emmerson and Lord Radstock had died some years earlier. Patty lived on at Northborough for another seven years and died in 1871 at the age of 72. She was buried, not at Helpston, near her husband, but in Northborough churchyard, next to her four children and other members of the family. The last main characters in the life of John Clare had also reached the end of their earthly pilgrimage.

In June 1989 a memorial plaque to Clare was unveiled in Poets' Corner, Westminster Abbey. The memorial bears the inscription 'Fields were the essence of the song.' His poetry has recreated for a new generation that paradise he had known as a boy – a world of innocence, hope, joy and celebration against the tragic background of his poverty, illness and despair that led to his mental breakdown. 'A Vision', written in the Northampton asylum in 1844, sums up the whole story better than any other words could do:

> I lost the love of heaven above
> I spurned the lust of earth below
> I felt the sweets of fancied love
> And hell itself my only foe.

I lost earth's joys but felt the glow
Of heaven's flame abound in me
Till loveliness and I did grow
The bard of immortality.

I loved but woman fell away
I hid me from her faded fame
I snatched the sun's eternal ray
And wrote till earth was but a name.

In every language upon earth
On every shore, o'er every sea,
I gave my name immortal birth,
And kept my spirit with the free.[19]

Neglected for over a hundred years, John Clare is now receiving full scholarly recognition. He is widely taught in schools and universities, and he has become the subject of an abundance of books, articles and dissertations. The John Clare Society, whose membership includes people from all over the world, was founded in 1981 to promote a wider and deeper knowledge of the poet. It organises the annual Clare Festival in Helpston, and arranges exhibitions, poetry readings and conferences to reflect the growing interest in his life and work. It also aims to protect Helpston's environment and to conserve the English countryside for future generations. This is a fitting tribute to the Northamptonshire Peasant whose wish was that people would read his poetry, enjoy it, and associate it with the landscape that made it possible.

NOTES

1. Frederick W. Martin: *The Life of John Clare,* page 291
2. See Geoffrey Grigson's Introduction to *Poems of John Clare's Madness,* page 22
3. Martin: *The Life of John Clare,* page 292
4. Mark Storey (ed.): *The Letters of John Clare,* page 654
5. J.W. and Anne Tibble: *John Clare: A Life,* page 373
6. June Wilson: *Green Shadows: The Life of John Clare,* page 253
7. *John Clare by Himself,* page 271
8. *The Oxford Authors: John Clare,* page 291
9. Geoffrey Summerfield (ed.): *John Clare: Selected Poetry,* page 291
10. *The Oxford Authors: John Clare,* page 361
11. Mark Storey (ed.): *The Letters of John Clare,* page 650
12. *Ibid.* page 657
13. *The Oxford Authors: John Clare,* page 427. The John Clare addressed here is probably Clare's son, but the image is of his own youth.
14. J.W. and Anne Tibble: *John Clare: A Life,* page 223
15. Mark Storey (ed.): *The Letters of John Clare,* page 683
16. *The Oxford Authors: John Clare,* page 427
17. *John Clare by Himself,* page 246
18. Mark Storey (ed.): *Clare: The Critical Heritage,* page 272
19. Geoffrey Summerfield (ed.): *John Clare: Selected Poetry,* page 274

Chronology

1793	John Clare born at Helpston, 13th July. His twin sister dies.
1795	Keats born. Speenhamland system of poor relief introduced.
1797	Mary Joyce born.
1798-*c.*1806	Attends schools at Helpston and Glinton.
1799	Martha (Patty) Turner born.
*c.*1800	First meets Mary Joyce.
1804	Napoleon proclaimed Emperor.
*c.*1806	Works as ploughboy for Mrs Bellairs at Woodcroft Castle.
*c.*1809	Works for Francis Gregory at the Blue Bell Inn, Helpston.
1809	Act of Parliament passed, 'for enclosing lands in the parishes of Maxey with Deepingate, Northborough, Glinton with Peakirk, Etton, and Helpstone'.
*c.*1810	Apprentice gardener for the Marquis of Exeter at Burghley House.
*c.*1812	Enlists in local militia.
1814	Buys his first 'blank book' from J.B. Henson, Market Deeping bookseller.
1814-1817	Makes acquaintance of gypsies.
*c.*1816	Relationship with Mary Joyce ends.
1817	Works as limeburner for Wilders at Bridge Casterton. First courts Elizabeth Newbon and later Martha Turner.
1818	Issues a proposal for publishing by subscription which catches the attention of Edward Drury, John Taylor's cousin.
1819	Becomes friendly with Isaiah Knowles Holland and Octavius Gilchrist. Introduced to the London publisher

	John Taylor; arrangements made for publication of first volume.
1820	*Poems Descriptive of Rural Life and Scenery* published on 16th January. Marries 'Patty'. Clare visits London for the first time. Portrait painted by William Hilton. Subscription list started on initiative of Lord Radstock and Taylor.
1820	Anna Maria Clare born on 2nd June.
1821	Fourth edition of *Poems Descriptive of Rural Life and Scenery*. 'Sketches in the Life of John Clare by Himself' completed. *The Village Minstrel* published.
1822	Second visit to London. Eliza Louisa Clare born on 13th June.
1823	Finishes *The Parish* (unpublished in his life-time). Second edition of *The Village Minstrel* published. Death of Octavius Gilchrist. Plans for *The Shepherd's Calendar* mooted by Taylor and Hessey.
1823-1825	Spells of prolonged and severe illness.
1824	Death of Byron. Frederick Clare born. Third visit to London; gets medical help from Dr Darling.
1824-1825	Keeps regular journal.
1826	John Clare (son) born.
1827	*The Shepherd's Calendar* published.
1828	Visits London for relief of depression. William Parker Clare born. Visits Boston, Lincs. Does field-work until 1831.
1829	Receives accounts from Taylor and Hessey. Takes issue over accounts with Taylor and Drury.
1830	Sophia Clare born.
1830	Severe illness.
1832	Reform Act. Moves to Northborough to a cottage provided by Earl Fitzwilliam.
	Writes 'The Flitting'. Proposals printed for *The Midsummer Cushion*.

1833	Charles Clare born.
1833-1835	Increasing illness and despondency.
1834	Poor Law Amendment Act.
1835	*The Rural Muse* published. Clare's mother dies.
1836	Suffers lapses of memory and delusions.
1837	Enters Dr Matthew Allen's asylum at High Beach, Epping Forest as a voluntary patient.
1838	Mary Joyce dies.
1840	Reports in newspapers of Clare's death.
1841	Writes 'Child Harold' and 'Don Juan'. Escapes from High Beach; walks back to Northborough; writes account of the 'Journey out of Essex'. Removed to Northampton General Lunatic Asylum.
1842-1850	William F. Knight transcribes Clare's poems.
1843	Frederick Clare dies.
1844	Anna Maria Clare dies.
1846	Clare's father dies.
1850	W.F. Knight leaves Northampton for Birmingham.
1852	Charles Clare dies.
1864	Clare dies at Northampton, 20th May. Taylor dies 5th July.
1865	Frederick Martin's *Life of John Clare* published.

Select Bibliography

PUBLISHED EDITIONS OF CLARE'S WORKS

Poems Descriptive of Rural Life and Scenery, a reprint of the fourth edition of 1821 (Lark Publications, 1986)

The Shepherd's Calendar, ed. Eric Robinson, Geoffrey Summerfield and David Powell (Oxford University Press, 1964. Second Edition, 1993)

The Rural Muse, ed. Kelsey Thornton (Mid-Northumberland Arts Group and Carcanet Press, 1982)

The Parish, ed. Eric Robinson (Penguin-Viking, 1985)

The Midsummer Cushion, ed. Kelsey Thornton and Anne Tibble (Mid-Northumberland Arts Group and Carcanet Press, 1979)

Selected Poems and Prose of John Clare, ed. Eric Robinson and Geoffrey Summerfield (Oxford University Press, 1967)

John Clare: Selected Poems, ed. J.W. and Anne Tibble (J.M. Dent, 1965)

John Clare: Selected Poetry, ed. Geoffrey Summerfield (Penguin, 1990)

The Oxford Authors: John Clare, ed. Eric Robinson and David Powell (Oxford University Press, 1984)

John Clare: Love Poems, ed. Simon Kovesi (Bangkok: M & C Services, 1999)

John Clare by Himself, ed. Eric Robinson and David Powell (Mid-Northumberland Arts Group and Carcanet Press, 1996)

John Clare: The Living Year 1841, ed. Tim Chilcott (Nottingham Trent University: Trent Editions, 1999)

The Letters of John Clare, ed. Mark Storey (Oxford: Clarendon Press, 1984)

The Early Poems of John Clare, ed. Eric Robinson, David Powell and Margaret Grainger (Manchester University Press, 1984)

John Clare, Poems of the Middle Period 1822-1837, ed. E. Robinson, D. Powell and M. Grainger. (Oxford: Clarendon Press, Vols I-II, 1996, Vols III-IV, 1998)

The Later Poems of John Clare, ed. Eric Robinson, David Powell and M. Grainger (Oxford: Clarendon Press, 1984)

John Clare, the Poet and the Place, poems illustrated with photographs by Peter Moyse, Peterborough 1993

CRITICAL AND BIOGRAPHICAL WORKS

Barrell, John, *The Idea of Landscape and the Sense of Place, 1730-1840: An Approach to the Poetry of John Clare* (Oxford University Press, 1972)

Brownlow, T., *John Clare and the Picturesque Landscape* (Oxford University Press, 1980)

Chilcott, T., *A Real World and a Doubting Mind: A Critical Study of the Poetry of John Clare* (Hull University Press, 1985)

Clare, Joanne, *John Clare and the Bounds of Circumstance* (Kingston and Montreal: McGill-Queen's University Press, 1987)

Deacon, George, *John Clare and the Folk Tradition* (Sinclair Browne Ltd, 1983)

Grigson, Geoffrey, *Poems of John Clare's Madness* (Routledge & Kegan Paul, 1949)

Haughton, H., and Phillips, A., (eds.) *John Clare in Context* (Cambridge University Press, 1994)

Martin, Frederick W., *The Life of John Clare* (Macmillan, 1865. Second Edition with Introduction and Notes by Eric Robinson and Geoffrey Summerfield: Frank Cass, 1964)

Storey, Edward, *A Right to Song: The Life of John Clare* (Methuen, 1982)

Storey, Mark, *The Poetry of John Clare: A Critical Introduction* (Macmillan, 1974)

Storey, Mark (ed.), *Clare: The Critical Heritage* (Routledge & Kegan Paul, 1973)

Tibble, J.W. and Anne, *John Clare: A Life* (London: 1932; revised edition 1972)

Wilson, June, *Green Shadows: The Life of John Clare* (Hodder & Stoughton, 1951)

Index

THE JOHN CLARE SOCIETY

Readers may wish to know about the John Clare Society, which was founded in 1981. Its aims are to bring together all lovers of his poetry and prose who find him 'a voice for our time'. Further details are available from the Hon. Secretary: Mr Peter Moyse, The Stables, 1A West Street, Helpston, Peterborough PE6 DU. Tel: 01733 252678.